We Be Jammin

We Be Jammin
Liberating Discourses from the Land of the Seven Flags

Eliseo Pérez Álvarez

foreword

by

Justo L. González

LUTHERAN SCHOOL
OF THEOLOGY AT CHICAGO

CENTRO
BASILEA
DE INVESTIGACIÓN
Y APOYO. A.C.

© Publicaciones El Faro S.A. de C.V.
Abasolo 93, Colonia del Carmen
04100 Coyoacán, México, D.F.

© CCGM
The Chicago Center for Global Ministries (CCGM) is an ecumenical
venture of Catholic Theological Union (CTU), Lutheran School of
Theology at Chicago (LSTC) and McCormick (Presbyterian Church,
USA) Theological Seminary (MTS).

© Lutheran School of Theology at Chicago
Hispanic/Latino Ministry Program
(773)256-0700
www.lstc.edu

© Centro Basilea de Investigación y Apoyo, A.C.
Francisco Fernández del Castillo No. 2509
Col. Villa de Cortés, Deleg. Benito Juárez, 03530 México, D.F.
cbasilea@hotmail.com

© 2002 by Eliseo Pérez Álvarez
dreperez@seminarioevangelicopr.org
Printed in México

Cover illustrations: Buddoe (Moses Gottlieb), West Indies liberator.
Ginger Thomas, national flower. Bitter sugar mill. Sunrise at the
Caribbean Sea.

Cover art: Paul Youngblood
Cover design: Gina Gabriela Pérez Dorantes
Text design and composition: Rodolfo Espinosa Ceballos
Indexes: Isaac Omar Espinoza Jiménez
Printer: Jiménez Editores

ISBN 968-7197-66-8

Printed in Mexico, 2002

To my parents

Eliseo Pérez Jacobo
(May 26, 1910 - Sep 18, 1992)
&
Catalina Álvarez Díaz
(January 8, 1926)

My first mentors in the following of Jesus.

To
Kingshill Lutheran Church
&
Christus Victor Lutheran Church
St. Croix, United States Virgin Islands

For being a balm in Gilead,
for making the wounded whole,
for healing the sin-sick soul.

Table of Contents

VIII

Acknowledgments

I would like to start by stating my loving appreciation to my wife Regina for her encouragement, proofreading and valuable criticism during these years of preaching in a second language. By the same token, my aunt Esther Shank, a dietician and convinced Mennonite pacifist, gave her blessing to this book as well: "your liberation theology comes out loud and clear —not oblique or hidden— especially in your slight changes in the liturgy 'God our Father and Mother', 'God our Liberator', etc."

A couple of pastors have told me that to travel every week in those small airplanes to do pulpit supply is kind of like a sacrifice. Nothing further from the truth. My deep appreciation goes to Bishop Francisco Sosa, "Paquitín" for inviting me to perform this sacred task of preaching Jesus Christ's liberating gospel in the fascinating culture of the USA Virgin Islands.

Deaconess Thelma Youngblood, my collegue. I appreciate her enlightened conversations and her enthusiasm in this publication. I also owe her the exquisite art of the cover, painted by her son Paul Youngblood.

Ediberto López, a New Testament scholar of the Seminario Evangélico de Puerto Rico deserves my gratitud for his reading of the manuscript. His sharp reactions forced me to revisit some sermons. Yet, I assume full responsibility for the content of the same.

This is the appropiate place to retrace my friendship for decades with Rodolfo Espinosa Ceballos, pastor, art designer and publisher. And, last but not least, I thank Ing. Abel Plata

Orozco, Director of "El Faro," the 117 year- old Presbyterian publishing house. He not only donated one of his kidneys to a nephew, he gives of himself by spreading the word of God through the printing press.

XII

Preface

Cross-cultural communication is one of the foci of the Chicago Center for Global Ministries. The church has and will always proclaim Jesus Christ in new languages, symbols and insights. Every new context demands dynamic re-thinking of the preaching of Jesus. We are convinced that the church will speak creatively in new voices or it will not participate in the Mission of God.

As the early church was driven out of Jerusalem and into the regions of Judea and Samaria, the disciples spoke and served in the Aramaic language. Their Judean and Galilean cultures molded their proclamation of the gospel. Jesus was proclaimed as the Messiah or the Coming Messiah who fulfilled all of the dreams of the ancient prophets or as the Son of Man who would one day appear in the clouds of heaven as had been envisioned by the prophet Daniel. However, within a generation a majority of the "followers of the way" were Greek speaking inhabitants of the Roman Empire. They represented an ethnic and cultural diversity bound together by a political structure which was headed by an emperor designated as "dominus and deus" or lord and god. In this new context the New Testament was written not in Aramaic, but in Greek, and Jesus was proclaimed in absolute opposition to this political power as Lord and God. The church down though the centuries has mined every new context, every new culture for language and wisdom to preach Jesus as the Christ or Lord or Son. And at its best it has challenged all authorities which are in opposition to the Reign of God.

It is for this reason that we are delighted to co-sponsor the publication of this new volume of sermons from the Island of St.

Croix in the Virgin Islands. The sermons of Dr. Eliseo Pérez Álvarez sparkle with new images and visions as this Mexican pastor and theologian strives to preach the gospel in the island world of the Caribbean. We are invited into a community, birthed in slavery and still struggling for life and justice, but where the joy of faith overcomes the world.

Mark Thomsen
Director of the Chicago Center for Global Ministries

XIV

Pre-lude

Before we start lauding (worsiping) God through the following sermons, I would like to say that this book is a collection of discourses by Dr. Eliseo Pérez. They are a definite challenge to incorporate the culture and history of the Land of the Seven Flags from a biblical and black perspective.

It is the purpose of this collection of discourses to enrich, ennoble and encourage our spiritual growth and development, as well as historical understanding of events in the Caribbean.

Dr. Eliseo Pérez, a very gracious and humble professor at the Seminario Evangélico de Puerto Rico, was assigned by the Rev. Francisco Sosa, Bishop of the Caribbean Synod to serve the vacant Kingshill and Christus Victor Lutheran Congregations as a Vice Pastor in October 1998. From the outset he showed himself to be a very sensitive and committed hard worker in the Lord's Kingdom. These are a collection of some of the sermons he delivered to the congregation from 1998 to 2001.

We wish you will find them a source of inspiration and spiritual awakening. It is my sincere hope that you will be touched and blessed by these discourses.

Thelma Youngblood, Deaconess
Christiansted, St. Croix, USVI, June 24, 2001
Saint John the Baptist's Day

Foreword

Preaching has always been a central activity of the church. This is not just because it is an ancient and tried means of communication. It is also because the church is the people of the Word. Our God is a God who speaks. Indeed, our God's speech is so powerful, that through God's speech—God's Word—all things are made, and without such speech nothing has been made (Jn 1.3).

In the church, we speak not only because we are human beings who must communicate, but also because we are the people of the God who speaks. We speak in service and in response to God's Word. We also speak trusting that, through God's inexplicable grace and by the power of the Spirit who is God, the Word of God will become incarnate in our words, use them as God's Word for us and for the entire church, and thus bring about a new creation, a birth as radically new as the very first creation.

For these reasons, a sermon is not merely a speech, an address, a lecture, an exhortation. A sermon is a plea to the God of the church, that our words be taken up by the Word, and create a new thing.

For the same reasons, a sermon is not merely a text. I would even venture to say that the written text that we often call a "sermon" is not such. It is the *text* of a sermon; but it is not the sermon itself. A sermon, more than a text, is an event. The *sermon* —word— is in the activity of the Word of God when the words of the preacher, taken up by the Spirit, are being heard by the congregation in such a way that there is indeed a new creation, a new reality, a new way of being, a new way of understanding, a new way of relating. A sermon, like any human word, is not truly a word unless it is both spoken and heard, uttered and received.

Since human words are taken up by the Word, not on the basis of their value, eloquence, or accuracy, but merely on the basis of God's graceful and sovereign decision, the preacher cannot guarantee that such a momentous event will indeed take place. My words are always my words, and no more, until God takes them up and uses them. I cannot claim that, because I crafted my sermon, or because I studied diligently, or because I spoke eloquently, God will take up my words into the Word.

All that I can do—and therefore, what I *must* do—is do my best so that my words are congruent with the Word who was made flesh in Jesus Christ. I offer my words as my best offering, hoping and praying that God will take up what little I can do, and infuse it with power. In reading and studying a scriptural text for a sermon, I must seek to understand what it might mean for us today, and to express it with as much clarity and force as I can. And yet, the true clarity and force of the sermon will not be mine nor depend on me, but will be God's and be the result of God's action.

In thus seeking to make my words congruent with God's Word for us today, I must perform two tasks—both necessary if I am to be obedient to my calling, and yet neither sufficient without the action of the Spirit bringing the Word to us.

The first such task—although not chronologically distinct from the second—is to seek to understand the Bible in general, and the particular biblical passage specifically. That is both a devotional and an exegetical task.

It is a devotional task, because it does not suffice to understand the meaning of the words in a passage, or even the meaning of the passage as a whole. It is also necessary that we become a "biblical people"—not in the sense that we know the Bible by heart, or that we set up a series of "biblical" rules for life, but

XVIII

rather in the sense that our entire life, both as individuals and as a community, is shaped by the Word of God. Although good exegesis is important, this cannot be done by mere exegesis, no matter how scientific, careful, or detailed. It is rather a devotional matter; a matter of discipline; a matter of allowing Scripture so to judge and form us, that we become more truly "biblical" in the deeper sense. Without this placing ourselves and our communities of faith under the scrutiny of Scripture, there is no point in placing Scripture under the scrutiny of exegesis. One could summarize this by saying that biblical wisdom is a necessary foundation for biblical preaching.

There is also, however, an exegetical dimension to this first task of seeking to understand the biblical passage we are about to preach. For this, good will and devotion do not suffice. Wisdom must be joined to knowledge. The same Scripture which we read devotionally, placing ourselves under its scrutiny, must also be read under the serious scrutiny of all the exegetical tools at our disposal. Faithful biblical preaching is not simply a matter of choosing a few words that for some reason strike our fancy, and then jumping into whatever we feel like saying, or into religious and spiritual platitudes. As has often been said, true biblical preaching does not use the text as a pretext.

Thus, the first task before a preacher who wishes to be faithful is to take the text of Scripture seriously, and from it to derive both wisdom and knowledge.

The second task is to build a bridge between that ancient word and today's challenges, anxieties, doubts, hopes—in short, today's life. Just as the Word did not become incarnate in a "general" human being, but in the concrete, historical, particular, Jesus of Nazareth, so today the Word does not speak in generalities, or to "humankind" in general, but is made flesh in the concrete sermon preached in a particular historical circumstance, within a particular culture, etc

XIX

The first of these two tasks seeks to insure the *textual* basis for the sermon—that my words are grounded on the Word. The second is its *contextual* dimension.

The sermon texts that form this book are excellent examples of how these two tasks can be performed. Their exegetical and textual integrity will be obvious to any reader. These sermons were grounded on Scripture, which they took very seriously. The exegesis is sound, although not always apparent, but implicit—as indeed it should usually be.

However, what is most striking about the pages that follow is their contextuality. These are clearly sermons, not just on a particular text of Scripture, but also preached in a particular context, within a particular congregation, in a particular culture.

This is not just textual preaching—which unfortunately has been much neglected in many of our churches—but also contextual preaching—which unfortunately has also been much neglected.

Clearly, all preaching, like all human existence and thought, is contextual. The most "generic" sounding sermon reflects a context—or rather, a constellation of contexts. A "sermon" without a context is not a sermon at all. It is a series of words. It is like an event without time or place. It simply does not happen.

For these reasons, the sermons whose written texts comprise this book cannot be repeated, even though their words may be read once and again. A true sermon is not repeatable, just as no event is truly repeatable. These were sermons preached at a particular time, in a particular setting, and clearly addressing a very particular cultural context. And therein lies their value for preachers and others in all kinds of different settings.

In their clear, concrete, and even limiting contextuality, these texts have a greater universal value, precisely because if there is one universal characteristic of all good preaching it is contextuality. Those who read the pages that follow will not find in them sermons they

XX

can preach in their own contexts and places. What they will find is rather a testimony to and an example of excellent contextual and exegetical preaching, and a call and an invitation to engage their own contexts with a similar passion and creativity.

Dr. Eliseo Pérez-Álvarez, the author of this book, is himself an example of how contextuality may be practiced and affirmed even across cultural and linguistic borders. Himself a Mexican, during the course of his studies in Atlanta, Chicago and Denmark, he had the experience of his own recontextualization into the Hispanic-American or Latino community. Teaching in the Evangelical Seminary of Puerto Rico, he experienced still another recontextualization. Thus, his freedom and creativity in engaging the context of the Virgin Islands, and his appreciation of that context, should come as no surprise to us. But they do come as a valuable gift to any who are struggling with the function of preaching today, and the shape it should take.

Justo L. González
Decatur, Georgia
October 4, 2001 (Day of the Feast of St. Francis)

XXI

Introduction

I became acquainted with the United States Virgin Islands through my reading of Danish theologian and philosopher Søren Kierkegaard. By mid XIX century Regina Olsen, Kierkegaard's ex-fiancé, married the West Indies' governor and she ended up living in these lands. The subtitle of this book is also derived from Kierkegaard's different collections of sermons which he entitled "Edifying Discourses." However, they were in fact "liberating discourses." In a *Journal* entry which is worthwhile quoting at length our Nordic preacher noticed the link which exists between the bourgeois way of life and the moral validation provided by the clergy:

Let us assume that it became customary for a clergyman to have a business manager who would collect his money, tithes, offerings, etc., which is quite all right inasmuch as the business manager is in the clergyman's service. But let us suppose that this became an independent way of making a living and that such a business manager would pay the clergyman his wages and now himself made the plans and had only a financial interest in the pastor's standing with the congregation. What then? Well, this would result in the practice that the pastor, every Saturday night upon finishing his sermon, would go over to the business manager and let him see it. And the business manager would say: 'If your Reverence talks this way, no one will come to church, and, damn it all, there goes the offering plate money, and in that case I can't guarantee much for this year, which, after all, is to your own interest. No, you must butter up the congregation a little; let me tell you how. If I am not quite up to writing a sermon, I do understand very well the times we live in and what the congregation wants.'

*I imagine the pastor would flush with embarrassment and say:
'Have I been appointed teacher in order to flatter the congregation
and for you to earn money?' But the business manager answers:
'I have no time for hysterics, high-mindedness, and all that.
Everyone is a thief in his own job, and my job is to see to it that
Your Reverence satisfies the times.'*

*The nauseousness of the moneyman's sniffing at the sermon
and judging it commercially is revolting enough (Pap VII 1 A
77 n.d., 1846) (Hong, 2767).*

It is a bad line to affirm that the Bible is God's word. Nevertheless,
the Bible is a double-edged sword. This Sacred Book has been
used through the milleniums to domesticate the spirits and bodies of
some segments of society. But also our Holy Scriptures have been a
source of emancipatory movements. "Liberating discourses" seek
to do justice to the Gospel of Jesus Christ, which addresses reality
from the point of view of freedom. The doctrines of the sacraments,
of the church, of salvation, etc., are to be interpreted through the
liberating teaching and doing of the Nazarene.

Liberating Discourses have the open agenda of reading the Bible
from the socio-economic and political perspective. Instead of
interpreting the Scriptures from a privatistic, spiritualistic, or
ahistorical way, my approach is engaged with a holistic liberation:
spiritual, physical, political and cosmical. In a sense, this book is a
counterpart of the chapter on homiletics methodology I wrote in
Christian Pulpit and Social Justice.[1]

This book of discourses does not follow the typical structure of a
sermon. My goal is to draw alternative avenues in our study of the
Bible. In doing so, I have tried to be sensitive to the USVI culture,
to honor my social location as people of color, and to address the
everyday reality.

"We be jammin" is a Caribbean expression that suggests mingling,
dancing, getting together, celebrating, experiencing liberation! Even

in Puerto Rico people sing: "¡Qué jammeo papá!"[2] pointing towards a life of plenty, of dignity, of freedom.

In jazz jargon, to jamm means to create a melody from scratch, to improvise, to stick in the melodic ocean with the particular wave of your musical instrument. "We be jammin" is the empowerment I have experienced from the hospitable Caribbean to make my contribution to the concert of life.

During my first visit to St. Croix I felt everything was going my way. Pretty soon I realized I was driving in the wrong lane! My first reaction was: "why don't these Virgin Islanders drive the logical way, that is, in the right lane?" This was a typical ethnocentric temptation. Instead of celebrating the Other, the different one, we are prone to our own cultural supremacist interpretation.

It has been an honor to share my weekends with the people from the Land of the Seven Flags. This is a place of courageous brothers and sisters who have been tempered by the huricanes, originated by natural causes and also provoked by rapacious imperialistic countries. This is an Island of warm folks. I have been so fortunate in getting to know their people, their dishes, their dances, their way of driving on the left lane, their way of fixing things, their sense of humor.

In 25 years of preaching I never had so many theological conversations with parishioners as in St. Croix. These warm hearts, together with a tiny few work in editing these meditations made this publication possible.

I hope you like jammin too!

Río Piedras, Puerto Rico,
November 2001 XXV
Søren Aabye Kierkegaard Day

First Part

The Table

1
THE DISTANT AND THE CLOSE GOD
Psalm 113

Psalm 113 is a song of praise that Jews and Christians have favored in their worshiping. Jews sing this song in the feast of the Tabernacles, the feast of the Weeks and above all during the Passover.

Christians visit this hymn while celebrating the Eucharist and on Easter as well. Chances are that Jesus and his disciples sang Psalm 113 at the Last Supper: "And when they had sung a hymn, they went out to the Mount of Olives." (Mk 14.26)

Hallel—praise— or Halleluya—praise God, is but another name for this song. This psalm addresses God´s attributes and God´s deeds. Bible scholars associate Psalm 113 with the protest songs of Hannah (1 Sam.2.1-11) of the Old Testament, and the Magnificat (Lk1.46-55) of the New Testament.

This psalm mainly portrays God's farness and God closeness, or what is known in theology as God's transcendence and God's immanence:

I. The Distant God, 4-5
The State's general interest are more closely linked with the welfare of the company (Schimmelmann).

Count Ernst Schimmelmann (1747-1831), was a Danish Minister of Finance who was a large plantation owner and a slave trader. In Denmark he was known as the patron of poets, but in the West Indies he was practically known only by the state managers. In 1763 Count Schimmelmann inherited from Henrich Carl von Schimmelmann Royal plantations and slave holdings on the islands of St. Croix, St. Thomas and St. John. Count Schimmelmann continued the European typical tradition of distant, absentee-landlords.

On the contrary, God does not want to be in the company of the mighty and tyrannic rulers of the world. God distances Godself from the kings and queens who behave as if God didn´t exist. God reveals Godself in God's highness in order to take distance from the idols and tyrants that have replaced God. God's aboveness is the landmark of his disagreement with the people, countries or structures that have denied God's love and justice.

That is precisely the meaning of the Reformation of the 16th century and the reformations of the Christian church that have taken place throughout history. The distant God is not an insensitive God disconnected from the world. Quite the opposite. The distant God is the God who does not agree with the earthly order of things, and who continues teaching us how to pray: "Your will be done on earth as it is in heaven."

God is far from everybody and everything that dares to take God's place. However, God is close to the lowly, the sick, the captive, the oppressed, the poor and the needy. God opts for the poor, for the people who society considers superfluous.

And that is precisely the other huge discovery of the Reformation of the 16th century. The doctrine of justification by faith meant that God is near to each of us, who cares for us personally, even though we do not have the economic means to buy indulgences, and an endless number of church and society burdens.

St. Croix has been a suffering land for ages. This is an island that has changed flags for seven times since 1493 when the Europeans took possession of this paradise: Spain (1493-1650),

4

England (1587, 1625, 1642, 1646, 1801, 1807, 1815), Holland (1625), France (1625, 1649, 1650, 1733), Denmark (1733-1917), Knights of Malta (1651), USA (1917-).

Some people and some countries have the bad manners of rebaptizing everything. Joel R. Poinsett, a USA ambassor in Mexico changed the name of the flower *Cuitlaxochitl* (shrivel flower) to *Poinsettia*. Louis Antoine de Bougainville, the French navigator, stamped his last name *Bougainvilla* in a Brazilian flower. Puertorricans resisted and preferred to emphasize what it stands for, a Divine and human community: *Trinitaria*. European empires rebaptized the island of Ay Ay, as "Santa Cruz", "Holy Cross", "Het Heilig Kruis", Helige Kreuz and Saint Croix. Flags came and flags went, but the hard situation of the islanders remained the same. Ships like the Danish "Patriarch Jacob" drained the wealth of this beautiful place.

This biblical song also portrays:

II. God's Closeness 6-9

God stayed away from the absentee earthly landlords. Instead of that, God sent his son Buddoe to liberate the suffering people.

John Gottlieb Buddoe — also known through the oral tradition as Moses Gottlieb, or General Bordeaux— led an 8,000 slave uprising, together with Moses Robert and Martin King.

Buddoe showed up on horseback in the fort of Frederiksted by noon, July 3, 1848. Due to the extremely well planned rebellion, this skilled craftsman from *La Grange* plantation didn't have to recur to a bloody fight. Buddoe negotiated with the Governor, and in a peaceful way the great free slave strategist conquered emancipation from slavery for the whole population of the Danish West Indies.

5

Buddoe, the "Toussaint Louverture of St. Croix," was originally from the British Islands. He not only knew how to read and write, he also was aware of some of the long chain of the freedom fights from the sisters Caribbean islands: Hispaniola, 1522; Barbados 1649, 1816; Jamaica 1685, 1760, 1831; Antigua 1687, 1728, 1737, 1831; St. John 1733; Tobago 1770, 1771, 1774; Surinam 1763, 1772; British Guyana 1808, 1823; Guadeloupe 1802; Martinique 1822, 1831; Yare, Venezuela, 1747; Curazao 1750; Grenada 1795; Haiti, 1724, 1730, 1734, 1740; Saint Kitts and Nevis, 1725, the disbanded of Guiana's slaves, and so forth.

In order to diminish Buddoe's brilliance, some historians have told us that emancipation came from above. According to this, Buddoe has as co-conspirators either Governor Peter von Scholten or his mistress Anna Elizabeth Heegaard. She was a "very light-colored" or a "better-colored" lover who, according to Denmark's racist law, was prohibited to marry a white person. However, freedom came from below because von Scholten went back to Europe, Heegaard went back to her routine in St. Croix, whereas on July 6, Buddoe was arrested and imprisoned. On January 8, 1849 he arrived in Port-of-Spain, Trinidad, never to return.

In any event, God heard the cry of his people by sending this liberator's spirit back to St. Croix. This year of 1998 we are celebrating the 150 Anniversary of emancipation, and right now we can do our pilgrimage to Frederiksted Fort and realize that, right there in Buddoe Park stands the statue of our liberator. Buddoe's sculpture then is a constant reminder of God's closeness. Buddoe, like Moses, forced the Pharaoh to grant freedom to everybody.

6

Getting to the point:

St. Croix, as "the sugar king" made many foreigners rich, to the detriment of its own people. But God heard the cry of the people and remained close to the suffering islanders in order to alleviate their pains.

God —states psalm 113— has taken the side of the lowly. God has served the meal for them and has shown his closeness in this intimate dinner. In Jesus' time, as in some places of our own time, servants where not allowed to sit during their lunch time. Nonetheless, in this Eucharistic psalm, the Triune God, shows us not only his closeness but shows us God's desires for all of us to be seated at the table. For us to drink wine —not the daily Water (Is. 21.14). For us to drink in a cup —not in an ordinary glass. For us to eat fresh bread —not what Jews called sleepy bread, that is, bread that is old and hard, or stale bread.

Let us then praise God for being so distant from the tyrants and insensitive structures that kill people. Let us then praise God for being so close to the oppressed people. Let us mingle with God and with each other. We be jammin! Let's celebrate this 1998 Reformation Sunday feast. Come freely to the table as equals to participate of the body and blood of our Liberator Jesus Christ.

7

2
A NEW AGE OF HISTORY?
Galatians. 1.4, II Thessalonians 3.6-13

Every age has witnessed its own world order or better yet, disorder. The Assyrians, the Babylonians, the Persians, the Greeks, the Romans, the Spaniards, the Germans, etc. Currently we find the same idea in the one dollar US bills: *annuit coeptis* [God] has favored us, and *novus ordo seclorum* [USA] new age of history. But Gal 1.4 says that, in general, the world orders are evil and contrary to God's reign of justice, peace, brotherhood and sisterhood: "Jesus Christ has to rescue us out of the present evil order."

The reading of the epistle for this morning often has been misinterpreted. It has been entitled: "warning against idleness" and reduces the whole section to moral advice to stay away from idle persons, some even say, busybodies.

Rivers of ink have flown in an attempt to interpret this passage, trying to find the origin of idleness. Some argue that what Paul condemns is the thinking that the parousia was at hand. Consequently, people stopped working and were just waiting for Jesus' second coming. Due to the expectations of the imminent advent, many folks considered work as unnecessary. Because of this, many lived idle lives at the expense of the hard working classes.

A second explanation of this story tells us that what Paul is really rejecting is idleness in itself. From the outset a priority ministry of the Christian churches consisted of sharing the table with the hungry. During these communal meals, some just sat idly by and waited to be served. They were idle people who took advantage of the church's budget.

A third reading of the same paragraph points to the fact that the early Christian church was full of traveling preachers who were reluctant to work for their own bread (*Didache*). In contrast, taking for granted that Paul wrote 2 Thess, this third interpretation says, Paul introduced himself as an example of a tent maker and teacher who was not a burden on Christian communities (7,10).

One more reading of our Epistle passage emphasizes idleness due to the imminent return of Jesus. According to this, what Paul is actually condemning is the kind of people who, even though they are able to work, are unwilling to do so. "Anyone who is unwilling to work, shall not eat." Paul then exhorts, not the people who are unemployed, but the people who are positively refusing to work. Paul reminds them that he himself did not eat anyone's food without working for it. The fourth interpretation agrees in excommunicating this kind of idle person from the Christian fellowship: "In the name of our Lord Jesus Christ, stay away from every person who falls into idle habits." (3.6)

This morning, sisters and brothers, allow me to add an alternative interpretation. It is related to the fourth one, that speaks of people who remain idle against their will. Due to the lack of opportunity to earn their bread by the sweat of their brow, they have to remain inactive, unproductive, infertile. Actually, this is the tragedy of the end of this century. Some persons today are considered, by the people of power, not only idle but superfluous, completely unnecessary. This does not have to do with an unwillingness to work, but with the unfair order that, all of a sudden, throws millions of unemployed people out into the streets.

But I would like to propose to you something more. Right now, at the beginning of a new millennium, we have to think that, not only do there exist idle persons who eat their bread at the expense of the sweat of others, or people who work and are not able to enjoy the fruit of their labor, as Isaiah 65.22 says: "They [the poor people]

9

will not build for others to live in or plant for others to eat." Today, there exist hard working countries and continents which are not able to eat what they produce, and idle countries which eat the bread of hard working people. This is what is known as «the New Age of History.» But according to Gal 1.4 this is instead an "evil order" or a present world disorder.

The windmills that Deaconess Thelma has showed me all over the island, are mute witnesses to the millions of tables upon which St. Croix has put the «white gold.»

St. Croix, «the sugar king and queen» had famous merchants such as Sarah Roosevelt, John Hancock, the insurance company salesman, Abram Markoe, who gave up his home in Pennsylvania for the new site of the first White House. In St. Croix was also raised the African-American Alexander Hamilton, the first Secretary of the Treasury of the US. This Island was a potential sugar plantation for more then 200 years. In 1812 alone it exported 20,535 tons.

The "sugar money" had a great economic importance for Denmark. In the Copenhagen refineries it processed and exported sugar to Sweden, England, and other countries. For instance, Lord Macaulay said in 1845: "We import the accursed thing; we bond it; we employ your skill and machinery to render it more alluring to the eye and to the plate; we export it to Leghorn and Hamburg; we send it to all the coffee houses of Italy and Germany; we pocket a profit on all this; and then we put a Pharisaical air, and thank God that we are not like those sinful Italians and Germans who have not scrupple about swallowing slave-grown sugar."[3]

St. Croix's islanders can very well understand what our Epistle to the Thessalonians says about the people and countries that eat what they have not worked for, and the people and countries that can not eat what they produce. You yourselves have fed seven countries; as one can see the evidence of seven flags in central places. Allow me to mention some figures: The third world countries produce 80% of

10

the raw materials but consume only 7% of the world production. 300 million are permanently unemployed. 800 million have a daily income of about 30 cents on the dollar.

In the midst of this tragic landscape, the Holy Spirit is moving through people all over the world who are fighting for the cancellation of the immoral and unpayable foreign debts of all poor countries.

We Christians pray for this dream to come true after 500 years of experiencing how we cannot enjoy the fruit of our labor. We hope that we Christians never forget about Paul's excommunication of those countries that eat without having to work: "stay away from the people who fall into idle habits." We will continue to cry out in the streets and at the communion table for the overcoming of the present evil order and for the establishment of an order of justice and peace and solidarity with all suffering people.

11

3
UMBUMWE: THE COMMUNION OF THE SAINTS
Mark 1.29-34

Søren Kierkegaard, a Danish Lutheran pastor from the 19th century noticed that, we Christians made out of the Eucharist the real body of Christ, and we made out of the church the mystical body of Christ; whereas the early church did the opposite:

"The definition of «Church» found in the Augsburg Confession, as the communion of saints where the word is rightly taught and the sacraments rightly administered, quite correctly grasped only the two points about doctrine and sacraments and has overlooked the first, the communion of saints. Thus the Church is made into a communion of indifferent existences -but the «doctrine» is correct and the sacraments are rightly administered. This is really paganism."[4]

Now, the African-American way of reading the Bible takes us back to the origin: The Eucharist is the mystical body of Christ and the Church is the real body of Christ.

The Scripture passage for this Sunday tells us two things: the life of the physical body, and the communion with our neighbors:

I. The Life of the Physical body

St. Mark calls our attention to the fact that Jesus' ministry included the healing of many people. Jesus came in order to give life and life in abundance, this includes taking away all kinds of illness, because Jesus cares about our bodies.

The millenarian and rich African culture has known that for ages. The life of the body includes lively and rhythmic music, because as it is said: "this child was born dancing." Or if you prefer: "I hope you like a jammin too!" This art is created out of bottles and cans, clapping and humming, and of course, out of drums. Swinging our hips, moving our feet, forgetting completely about our arthritis. It is not by chance that during USA occupation of Haiti from 1915 to 1934, one of the main goal was to break the Hatian soul by burning their drums and prohibiting dancing and jammin, because according to USA, voodoo was a Satanic religion. Nothing further than the truth, as a recent survey discovered that in Haiti 95% are Roman Catholics and 150% practice voodoo. But both Jesus' culture and African culture include singing and jammin as a means to cure and celebrate the rights and the life of the body.

Together with that comes the body language. You can tell from a distance what African-American folks are talking about by the way they move their arms, their heads, their whole bodies. We can tell from a distance that Jesus is healing by the way he touches his sisters and brothers, by the way he took the hand of Peter's mother-in-law and lifted her up!

The love for bright colors like the sunshine as they are reflected in the paintings are so gratifying to the eye. This coming weekend St. Croix is going to host again the Agricultural feast. Folks from the sister islands will bring their art pieces, their food, their aromas, their music and dances. And everything will be done in order to celebrate the life of the body, "it feels good," "it looks cool," "it tastes great." Everything will remind us that the body has its own rights.

According to St. Mark, Jesus fed the people, Jesus made the people laugh, Jesus healed lots of bodies, because of the life of the bodies.

St. Mark also tells us about:

13

II. *Umbumwe*: Communion with our Neighbors
The entire life of Jesus was lived for the sake of others. This morning we find him healing many people. Jesus could very well

have said to himself, "you know, I already did many favors to this community, I'm gonna take a nap, or I wanna be alone, or I don't want anybody to bother me." But on the contrary, Jesus was always in communion with the people in need. In this case, Jesus took Peter's mother-in-law by the hand, and lifted her up!

The African-American culture also values so much *umbumwe*, the communion of the saints. Men get together and work in the house or in the field of a friend; women get together and help each other as well. Everybody gets together under a flamboyant shade and seals the *umbumwe*, the communion, with a meal.

When somebody of the community passes away, people are right there offering their help, bringing some food for everybody to get together and seal their *umbumwe*, their communion, with a meal.

In order to be able to face some economic responsibilities people enter a pool, a kind of savings among friends. In the Dominican Republic they call it *san*. On a weekly or monthly basis several families contribute a small portion of money to a common fund, and they chose a date for obtaining the whole amount of contributions and be ready to solve a problem through the *san*, or the umbumwe, the communion of the community.

The extended family is always open to receive a new guest for living with them because of work or study purposes. Other times people show *umbumwe* in raising other children who all of a sudden become orphans. Or in many cases the family is open to umbumwe, to communion with a guest that all of a sudden shows up for sharing the meal: "Today for you, tomorrow for me."

Umbumwe is what keeps Haitians alive in a country where each child is born 25 years old because of their short life expectancy. *Umbumwe*, communion, keeps them alive in a country where a child exploits the earth 280 times less than a child of the northern countries.

Umbumwe is what Jesus shows in lifting up this woman in Mark 1.31. But, according to Mark 15.21, umbumwe is what Simon from

14

Cyrene, a town from Africa, showed to Jesus in helping our Savior carry his cross!

Let us not Confuse the Mystical and the Real Body of Christ:
Let us continue celebrating the sacraments and preaching the word but the most important is the *umbumwe*, the communion of the saints. Our Sister Mayra Ballantine put it this way:
I do not claim to be self righteous,
Yet! I have these gifts within.
Caring, sharing and loving,
Giving to me from the One above.
Let us continue knowing Jesus Christ as he is found in the stories, songs, dances, poems, sermons, paintings, sayings of our people. But above all, let us continue knowing Jesus Christ in the umbumwe, in the communion of the saints, in his real presence through his church. May our church continue being a church that cares for the needs of the body, by being a church that creates scholarships, that supports people in need here in St. Croix and overseas, by being a church that, like Jesus Christ, takes people by the hand and lifts them up!

15

4
MANA FOR EVERYBODY!
Numbers 21.4-9

A few years ago while I was visiting the countryside in Arkansas, an elderly lady invited my wife, her aunt and I for Christmas dinner and offered me a slice of fruitcake for dessert, that she just remembered she had in her basement freezer. What was so shocking for me was that the fruitcake was 17 years old!

A cake 17 years old, I was telling myself. Wow! In many of our countries we buy, cook and eat food on a daily basis. The idea of storing food for days is unbelievable; our hunger gets rid of everything that is on the table. The concept of having seconds is out of the question. The idea of having a refrigerator packed with lots of goodies is simply beyond our imagination. And here I am, having before me a 17-year-old fruitcake! It was a finger licking-good cake, though!

The reading of the Old Testament for this 4th Sunday in Lent addresses this issue of eating and storing:

During the time of Israel's wandering through the desert the book of Numbers 11.4-9, 21.4-9 tells us that the people protested to God against the kind of food they were getting. As Ms. Bartley just read in v.5: "The people spoke against God and against Moses, ´Why have you brought us up out of Egypt to die in the desert? For there is no food and no water, and we detest this miserable food.´"

The people began to think about the manna which God provided for them. Then they started to raise these questions: Is manna really considered food? Isn't manna something boring?

Let's start with the first complaint:

I. Is Manna Really Considered Food?

For the Israelites, like for many of our cultures, to eat was to eat meat (Proverbs 15.17). They wanted meat, not some mere substitute! They forgot that in Genesis God, against God's own will, allowed people to start eating meat, but it was not the original plan of God as our teeth and digestive apparatus suggest. Instead of remembering that plan, they called manna "this miserable food."

I'm afraid things haven't changed very much. We have also learned that to eat means to eat meat. Some Spaniards that couldn't afford to eat meat used to walk on the streets with a toothpick in their mouths in order to make people believe that they had eaten meat for lunch! It is an open secret that more people can be fed with corn grains; but the meat business prefers to feed the cattle with corn and to feed the people with beef, which is extremely more expensive and less healthy! In some Caribbean countries there are people that can't afford to eat meat, but they themselves work for industries that manufacture pet food with high quality meat!

Let's pick up the second complaint:

II. Isn't Manna Something Boring?

The Israelites in the desert just got tired of such "miserable food."

Again, things haven't improved too much in our modern world since then. It is due to our boredom that we want to experience something new the whole time. It's due to our boredom that fruits, vegetables and animals have been shipped thousands of miles and still continue to travel long, long distances. For instance, the potato was originally from the Americas. Later, in 1586, Sir Francis Drake, the former pirate/lord, introduced the potato to Europe. Potato eventually saved Europe from starvation. Sugar traveled from the South Pacific islands, New Guinea, Philippines, Polynesia, to China,

17

to India, to the Canary Islands. Columbus then, on his 2nd voyage brought the "the white gold" to the Dominican Republic. And from there it arrived at St. Croix. From Africa came bananas and watermelon, among many other goodies.

Human beings just get tired of monotonous manna, and the food companies capitalize on that. In the desert the Israelites got poisonous snakes that bit them for rejecting God's manna. Today we have companies that burn the forests, arbitrarily set the international prices for food, pay a miserable wage to the agricultural workers, and continue poisoning the soil and the laborers with cancerous chemicals.

The exchange of vegetables, fruits and animals is fine. But what is not acceptable is that the food companies are not interested in feeding the people but in profiting with the marketing of food.

Allow me to take the third complaint of the Israelites in the desert:

Let me get it straight

People in the desert were not satisfied with such "miserable food," they longed for more and more and more food. Then their answer is no, manna is not enough.

They rejected the manna because it was perishable; it didn't last more than one day. Persons who attempted to store it found out by experience that manna got rotten. Manna is connected with the Lord's prayer: "give us today our daily bread." Manna is to be shared, otherwise it will spoil.

Our 20th century has developed tremendously in terms of science and technology. With modern industrialization, our planet has discovered how to get rid of manna as a perishable food and how to create new ways to store food. The invention of the refrigerator, the forcing of entire countries and islands to cultivate a single product, the changing of our taste by means of propaganda and of the availability of food, the precooked vacuum-packed meals which last from 5 to 21 days... many things tell us that while rejecting God's manna, hundreds of millions of people are dying of hunger.

18

The holy table thus, is a constant reminder that God's manna is still here on Earth. That God suffers in each person who suffers from hunger. That at God's table there's room for everybody.

What disturbed me a lot in Arkansas was the fact that while millions of people are starving, there are people that can store fruitcakes for 17 years.

In 1997 USA and Europe spent 17 billion dollars in food for pets!

The communion table is the permanent invitation for us Christian churches and members to share our bread with the needy.

The sacred book of the Egyptians, *The Book of Death,* mentions that in the last judgement one has to be able to say: "I never gave my back to a hungry person." In Matthew 25.35 Jesus says: "I was hungry and you fed me, thirsty and you gave me a drink" and Jesus continues: "I tell you, whenever you did this for one of the least important of these brothers and sisters of mine, you did it for me!"

19

5
THE GOD WHO CARNIVALS!
John 12.1-8

It took 2000 years for some people to realize that Jesus was not a Scandinavian man. The BBC (Brithish Broadcasting Company) of London, with the help of digital graphic technology, and with the skills of Richard Neave, a facial plastic surgeon of Manchester University, and Joe Zygas, an anthropologist, spent two years in rebuilding the face of Jesus. The more accurate picture of Jesus shows a man with prominent cheeks, pronounced nose, brown skin, and kinky hair.

The gospel of John of this morning adds something to the character of how Jesus is, which coincides with the research of the BBC. The God who carnivals with the poor.

Let me explain it, first:

I. The God Who Carnivals

Jesus is not like his cousin John the Baptist who fasted. Jesus is a "fiesta" man. Jesus is more a pre-lenten person, a carnival person. He just loves life; he celebrates life, he feasts, he parties, he be jammin!

If Jesus had incarnated in the Caribbean of the 21st century, he would be the first comer to carnivals like: Junkanoo and Goombay of Bahamas, Cop-Over of Barbados, Christmas Masquerades of St. Kitts and Montserrat, Jonkonnu of Jamaica, Hosay and Divali of Trinidad and Guyana, Rara of Haiti, and, of course, the Virgin Islands' Carnivals.

Still more. If Jesus had incarnated in the Caribbean 21ʳˢᵗ century, he would be the first attender at other festivities such as: the agricultural fair, art exhibitions in schools, crafts and food celebrations at the Whim Museum, music and cultural feasts at the Botanical Gardens, food banquets at the University of the Virgin Islands, jazzy afternoons at Kingshill Lutheran Church, calypso and reggae dances at Buddoe Park and all over the Island.

The new picture of Jesus of the BBC, is more likely to fit with the stories of our New Testament. Jesus just loved feasts because he knew that parties are not only important but they are an indispensable ingredient of our social livelihood.

Jesus knows that life is unbearable without "carnivaling." Jesus came for everybody to have an abundant life. All of us have been created for abundance and not for fatigue. There is a part within us that demands to be fulfilled. A calculating love is not really love. 300 denari represented one and a half times the annual salary of a Roman soldier. 300 denari represented the wages of more than three full years of a day worker.

The story of this morning has to do with a woman who, in annointing Jesus' feet with an expensive perfume, is really giving herself to Jesus without measure. She is not only going the extra mile, but she goes beyond the limits of reason, law and common sense! According to Judas, she is so wasteful. But what is the death of Jesus Christ on the cross if not the biggest of all wasteful events? Jesus could very well have avoided Jerusalem, he could have died a natural death at home surrounded by his dear ones. However, in this holy, wasteful act, Jesus gives himself on the cross without measure.

Mary's annointing of Jesus is pure extravagance!: 'the house was filled with the fragrance of the perfume" says the gospel. She spent lots of money for Jesus, and the book keeper Judas said: "that's a little too much for my taste," "that's not my cup of tea."

21

Now, let me go to the second point:

II. The God Who Carnivals with the Poor

Please, don't misquote me! I'm not promoting a style of life of "sun and fun." What I'm saying is that, Jesus, as a carpenter, as a bricklayer, as a fisherman, as a cook, knew first hand that life is unbearable without moments of celebration of life!

For people whose mode of life is "sun and fun," "no rum no fun," Jesus would tell them: "enough is enough" you better earn your bread by the sweat of your own brow!

But when Jesus preaches the abundance of life he is addressing poor people. Jesus is having dinner in Bethany, a poor village, in the poor home of his friends Lazarus, Mary and Martha. And let us always remember that Jesus himself was poor, as the BBC picture suggests! It is the poor that Jesus encourages to carnival, to party. It is the poor that Jesus reminds that they were created for a life of plenty and not for experiencing fatigue all the time.

How many Crucians do you know that besides their regular jobs they have to enlarge their pay check with a part-time job on weekdays, and another part-time job on weekends? To these brothers and sisters Jesus says, "hey, hold your horses, stop to smell the roses, fiesta time, carnival break, we be jammin!"

Carnivals and festivities are such a blessing in the midst of the monotony of steady tropical climate. That's why every Caribbean country has its major national festivals, which usually occur just before the season of Lent!

22

But the modern Judas still raises the criticism: what is in the Caribbean to celebrate besides the season of hurricanes and stuff if life is too harsh? How can that excessive amount of time, talent and money in preparing the carnivals be justified? What does the Carnival factor really mean to Caribbean emancipation?

Well, the gospel of this morning would answer those questions:

Carnivals are the major social process of "soul purging." Parades are like taking physical and psychological possession of the streets, specially the fancy streets where poor people are usually not allowed to walk. Parades are a liberating experience for the people where life is energized. While festing, the lines of social classification are blurred. For hard workers feasts mean a time of release, a time of abandonment to the spirits. To go to a feast is a way of affirmation. Listening to calypso and reggae is like listening to the voice of God! Life would be unbearable without those precious carnival days!

Let me put it this way:

On one occasion the African Anglican Bishop Desmond Tutu, peace novel prize winner, was in a meeting in England, where they happened to charge 10 cents for a cup of tea. Desmond Tutu offered to pay for the tea of a British gentleman who was looking for a dime. But the British was so reluctant: "Oh not at all, I'll pay myself because I don't want to be subsidized by anybody."

Well, this morning we find Jesus being subsidized not with a dime but with a huge amount of money which came from a poor woman.

Sisters and brothers, let "our houses be filled with the fragrance of Mary's perfume." Let us not be stingy with our time, our presence, our knowledge, our all as we share with the poor.

While carnivaling the physically challenged persons are healed 100%. While feasting time stops and the night is young. While partying, shy people feel freer to speak. While jammin, extravagant gifts and overwhelming love are bestowed. In the celebration of carnival, the big conquerors are ridiculed, people wear costumes of the conquerors but in a burlesque way. The feast enacts what our hymn reminds us of: "And now, let the weak say, 'I am strong,' let the poor say, 'I am rich,' because of what that Lord has done for us!"

All of that took place in the poor village of Bethany, in the poor home of Mary, Martha and Lazarus.

23

6
SOPHIA'S FEAST!
Proverbs 9.1-6

March is women's month. Therefore, allow me to honor half of humanity or half of heaven, by referring to the Jesus Christ of the table as a she.

One of the first titles for Christ was the Wisdom of God as it appears in 1 Cor 1. 22-24,30. It was a feminine title, Wisdom or Sophia. It is not surprising that the early Christian church referred very often to Proverbs 9.1-6 when they sat at the communion table.

In March women's month then:

I. It is a She Who Invites Us to the Feast. 1-2

Our hostess is waiting for us in her beautiful architectural house with 7 columns, the number of perfection. Her place is all fixed up for her guests: "Sophia has built her house and made seven columns for it. She has had an animal killed for a feast, mixed spices in the wine, and set the table."

This Eucharistic text of the Old Testament is not only pointing towards Jesus Christ as a she, as a Sophia of God. This passage of the Bible is also inviting us to honor women pastors and women bishops who, in the name of Sophia say to us: "Come, eat my food and drink the wine that I have mixed." Moreover, this biblical text also honors all those deaconesses, like Sister Youngblood, who Sunday after Sunday arrive early and leave late from church because they are busy preparing the loaf and the glasses. Proverbs 9 also connects the person who presides the table with all those anonymous women who for years and years have been setting the table by serving in the altar guild like Ms. Berryl Santos, Ms. Chi Thomas, Ms. Janice Knauzerburger, Ms. Naomi Alfred, Ms. Dolorita Davis, Ms. Doreen Rinas, Ms. Mary Shuster, Ms. Rita Spain, Ms. Sheris Isaac. In March, women's month then:

II. It is a She Who Invites Us to Share. 2-4
Sophia is calling everybody, especially the unschooled people, from the highest place in town. Everybody is included at her table. She cooked food and prepared very fine wine for everybody.

It is a she the one who tells us: "Come, eat my food and drink the wine that I have mixed." By the 5th century of the Christian church, the newest initiates who were baptized and had their first communion, were given a cup of milk sweetened with honey to symbolize the life and promise of God. Sophia's communion table is also a nourishing place with milk and honey to symbolize the richness of God. Sophia was certainly upset when in December 1993, in a mall of the US, a mother was arrested and evicted for breast-feeding her infant in public, and was charged with "indecent exposure."

Sophia is like the broken body of a mother in childbirth, the life-giving nature of brokenness. Sophia is happy every time a person is born and the table gets larger. The table is a symbol of invitation and reaches out to those who come into the church. And we, who are part of the church have to make other people feel very welcome here.

Prov 9. 3 "Sophia has sent her servant girls to call out from the highest place in town" reminds us of Luke 14.23: "Go out to the country roads and make people come in, so that my house will be full." St. Augustine, who was not so saintly, used this text to force Africans to become Christians aided by the use of the army. Centuries after, Europeans quoted the same text in order to force our ancestors to become Christians. But our text of Proverbs 9.3 is a lovely

25

invitation for everybody, especially the illiterate and poor people to become part of the Christian sharing and loving community: "Come, eat my food and drink the wine that I have mixed" says Sophia, or the feminine side of Jesus Christ.

Sophia, the Wisdom of God, reminds us that we Christians, are not only a spiritual community but a material community as well. I'm so pleased to see how every Lutheran church is requested to include in their yearly budget an amount for sharing with the most unfortunate people. I'm so proud to see how the Lutheran church in St. Croix promotes and supports social services. I'm so happy to see how they are involved in sharing its resources with people in need from the island and from overseas, too.

To be Christian is to follow the example of Sophia of sharing and loving, of calling everybody, especially the unschooled and needy people, from the highest place in town. Everybody is included at her table: "Come, eat my food and drink the wine that I have mixed."

To make the story short:
In March women's month then, it is Sophia Who Invites Us to Renew Our Knowledge. (9.10)

Sophia is at odds with women's sorry condition. Women earn salaries at least 25 % lower than men. 70% of people who live in misery are women. 65% out of the 1 billion illiterate people are women.

Sophia suffers by hearing Billy Graham, the most popular evangelist of the 20th century who wrote: "The biological assignment was basic and simple: Eve was to be mother, homemaker —this is the appointed destiny of real womanhood." And his wife, Ruth Graham, regarding women's ordination as pastors wrote: "I personally am against it. I believe that it basically goes against the principles of Scripture. I think if you study you will find that the finest cooks in the world are men; most of our greatest athletes are men. You name it, men are superior in all but two areas: women make the best wives and women make the best mothers."[5]

Sophia can't stand Germany's KKK. According to a German saying women are only good for Kinder, Küche and Kirche, that is, for children, kitchen and church!

The word *woman* comes from two words: wife and man, and when united formed *wifman*. In the 14th century it lost the f, forming *wiman*, and later changed into *woman*, that is, wife of men. *Female* comes from two Latin words: *fides* (faith) and *minus* (less), female means the one with less faith! Latin *mulier*, woman, comes from *mollitia*, which means weakness.

Sophia points in an opposite direction: "Wisdom begins with having reverence for God." Human knowledge is huge and everyday grows and grows but, human love is worse and worse because we look for human knowledge and not for Sophia, the Wisdom of God who involves the emotional intelligence as well.

On this Transfiguration Sunday let us give thanks to God for our women who have taught us how to be sharing and loving people. In order not to miss any women, we thank God for all of them as they are symbolized in our three centenarian St. Croix queens: Eliza McBean, Elsa Pedro & Elena Christian. And Sophia's feast goes on and on!

27

7

HE TOOK, BLESSED, BROKE AND GAVE BREAD![6]

John. 21.1-19

The table is the great theme of Jesus' ministry. This piece of furniture was surrounded by tension between communion and excommunion; between purity and impurity rules. Around the table slaves and women exercised their job of washing the guests' feet (Jn 13.2-11); around it the people fought for the chairs of honor in the seating arrangements (Lk 14.7-11); around it an endless list of eating habits was followed (Lk 7.44-46). And it is precisely at the table that Christians must discern the real presence of Christ (1 Cor 11) by giving preference to the shameful members of the body. (1 Cor 12.12-27)

The gospel story of this morning portrays Jesus as a cook, preparing a brunch by the sea for seven guests.

Some of Jesus' disciples spent the night fishing but their efforts were in vain. In the morning Jesus told them where to fish and they ended up getting 153 fishes. Jesus could very well have been disappointed with his disciples by deserting his call to become missionaries and catch human beings instead of fish. Nonetheless, Jesus wore an apron and assumed the role of a cook: he had ready a charcoal fire, he fried fish, had bread ready and started calling his disciples: "Hello!, brunch is ready."

This is so, because the Easter Jesus is feeding and serving us. At the table, in Jesus' culture, to take and to bless were male actions, whereas to break and to give were both female and servant actions. Let us take a closer look:

I. To Take and to Bless: Jesus is Feeding Us

To take and to bless were actions pertaining to the head of the family, to the father. Especially to bless or to give thanks was the privilege of the father of the family.

What John wants us to remember is that we Christians of the 21st century should never divorce the Holy Eucharist from the every day meal.

John the evangelist is writing at the end of the 1st century. Therefore he is addressing the third generation of Christians. By that time the Eucharist was a mere symbol, a mechanical celebration and who knows, perhaps also a superstitious sacrament.[7] That is why John doesn't mention the establishing of the Last Supper by Jesus. Instead of that, John reports the feeding of the crowd with 5 pieces of bread and 2 fish, and John also reports the resurrected Jesus' feeding of 7 disciples again with fish sandwiches!

Fish and bread was the basic diet of the Mediterranean people. Fish and bread was a basic meal for the Galileans. And most probably, every day, as Christians gathered together in the Galilean homes to eat fish and bread, they were reminded of the life and self-giving of Jesus Christ for everybody and everywhere.

Not surprisingly, Saint Augustine, in the 4th Century said: "when fish is fried Christ is sacrificed" (*Piscis assus, Cristus est passus*). However, in the same 4th Century, when Constantine, the emperor of the Roman empire, converted to Christianity, the meaning of fish was also converted.

Before Constantine, fish meant real food for Christians. After Constantine, fish means a symbol of salvation, but people would argue "salvation in what sense?" and the emperor would answer, "pie, pie in the sky, by and by" meaning, salvation in a future world, not salvation for right now! Salvation for the soul, not salvation for the body —don´t get any ideas!

The fish became a naive anagram (a word made by transforming

29

the letters of another word) Jesus Christ Son of God, Savior. It became a symbol of the born again Christians who had been baptized in the baptismal waters where fish live! After the collusion of the church with the empire, the fish no longer meant real food! More dangerous yet, after the domestication of Christianity by the emperor, the Holy Eucharist no longer was linked with the everyday eating of fish and bread! After the emperor the rule was: bread and wine in a symbolic way.

The image of Jesus as a cook who feeds his children was a little too much for the emperor whose official politics was: *panem et circenses*, that is, bread and circus; but whose politics in reality was: a lot of circus and no bread.

Now, let's go to the other two verbs:

II. To Break and to Give: Jesus is Serving Us

To break and to distribute bread was an accepted duty of women or servants.

Eating in Jesus' culture imitated the Greek and the Roman style with low tables, arranged in a U shape. Guests would recline on the left arm and use only the right hand for eating. Consequently it was impossible for the host to distribute the food by himself. What Jesus did was to break the bread and to give the food personally to the others. By doing so, Jesus played the role of women or servants!

Every time we have communion we are keeping alive those four strong verbs of the table. To take and to bless represents the role of the father, and to break and to distribute, the role of women or servants. It was not suitable for the father to break, to give, and some times even to take the bread, but Jesus is performing these tasks. What Jesus is really telling us is that, He is like the fried fish, that He is feeding us with his own life and that He is serving us as a servant, like the hard workers' wives or hard working women. And still more, Jesus, after serving everybody, served himself!

30

To Bring the Matter Closer:
In the confirmation class Dr. Ruth Beagles told us that sometimes Lutherans from St. Croix had to travel to St. Thomas to take communion. I'm so appreciative of the centrality of the table in the Lutheran tradition; nonetheless, we have to be aware of the implications of taking communion. Today we can think of at least two implications: to take and to bless bread means to feed, and to break and to give means to serve.

We need to relate the Holy Eucharist with the holy meals of everyday. Jesus is the fried fish who gives himself to others. We, his followers, should give ourselves to others too, in practical ways. In feeding them Jesus said: "because a poor person was hungry and you fed her or him, you did it to me."

The St. John Island slave uprising of 1733 is well-known for being one of the earliest Afro-American uprisings of the American Continent, but we have missed the point by not remembering that it was mainly motivated by the lack of food. Starvation was the main reason for the slaves running away from their masters.[8]

Last Thursday 100,000 people in the Old San Juan protested against the continuation of the bombarding of Vieques. The marines are killing people with the pollution and noise of the explosives which can be heard even from St. Thomas Island. The bombs are also killing fish, food not only of the Viequenses but also of Virgin Islanders and other islanders of our sister Caribbean countries! Those marines are from the same military corps that ruled the Virgin Islands from 1917 to 1931 "with an iron hand."

This Sunday there is no bombarding because in Rome the Pope is declaring Carlos Manuel Rodríguez the first Puertorrican local saint. You see, the marines are devoted Christians! On the mainland millions of people believe that Vieques is an uninhabited island. Even if the more than 9000 Viequenses didn't exist, what about the beautiful gray pelicans, other water birds, palm trees, the hills and valleys, and of course, what about fish?

31

President Bush says that what matters is "national security." The Viequenses argue that we have to distinguish between "national security" and "imperial security."

The big protesting crowd from the Old San Juan reminds us of the multitude spoken of in the gospel of John 6.14-15. Although it represented a social uprising for the Roman and Jewish authorities, Jesus went ahead and fed the crowd.

Sisters and brothers from all over our sister Caribbean islands which are also reached by WSTX radio station, we live in a cruel world where people are killed unnecessarily, where people go hungry because of irresponsible activities, where many wish to be served rather than to serve others. Take for instance the case of Dennis Titus, the billionaire who paid 20 million dollars to travel this week to the space station. He is the first space tourist to pay an exhorbitant fare for the first space taxi, instead of helping to feed the hungry. Many people and many churches just don´t care about taking, blessing, breaking and distributing bread. Many persons place their priorities in gaining honor and glory.

But the liberating news is that the cook Jesus Christ is on the side of the hungry. The liberating news is that the Christian church takes, blesses, breaks and gives bread to the hungry, to the suffering people, to the least and the last ones!

32

8
JESUS ATE BROILED FISH
Luke 24. 43, Psalm 95.5

Martin Niemoller, a German Lutheran pastor who opposed Hitler, warned us:

"In Germany first they arrested the communist; I didn't raise my voice because I wasn't a communist. Later they arrested the Jews; I didn't raise my voice because I wasn't a Jew. Later they arrested the commerce unionized workers; I didn't raise my voice because I wasn't unionized. Later they arrested the Roman-Catholics; I didn't raise my voice because I wasn't Roman-Catholic. Eventually they arrested me, and nobody was around in order to raise their voice..."

The psalm and the gospel for this morning tell us about the sea and about Jesus eating broiled fish. That reminds us about: The sea as the origin of life, and the sea as the preservation of life.

I. The Sea as the Origin of Life

In Jesus' time people had the idea of a three story house: heaven above, the Earth and the waters or the depth beneath the Earth (Ex 20.4).

The fact that the sea covers 3/4 of the planet and that we ourselves are pretty much the same percentage of water make scientists think life originated in the deepness of the sea 3,500 million years ago. Now we know that the sea is actually the thermometer of the world's weather. By way of retaining heat, it refreshes the Earth during the summer and warms it up during the Winter. The cultures from all over the world have told us about the sea, and that water is the basic element from which life emerges.

The novel of Ernest Hemingway: *The Old Man and the Sea* portrays the fisherman's love for the sea. When you're sailing or fishing in the midst of the sea you completely forget about land, about the clock. And the experience is more intense when it is dark. There is something magical and mysterious in the sea's womb that make us speechless.

The entire life of the world renowned Crucian captain "Bomba" Allick is also worth noticing. My namesake, Wilfred Elisha Allick, better known as "Bomba" was attached to the sea. At the age of 10 he was a cabin boy. At the age of 17 he became First Mate. At the age of 20 he was a captain! With the technology of 70 years ago he made a cross-Atlantic voyage to the Scandinavian countries, he fought several severe storms, and finally he was in the middle of the sea 48 hours prior to his death. No wonder three vessels have his name: "Bomba Charger," "Bomba Challenger" and "Bomba Cruiser."

Let's see now:

II. The Sea as the Preservation of Life

The Israelites had access to the Mediterranean, the Roman Lake, or the "great Sea" by way of some rivers. They also had the Dead Sea that was so salty that it contained no life. The only fresh sea water was the one from Galilee, also known as Lake of Gennesaret or Sea of Tiberias.

34

The Sea of Galilee had at least 19 species of fish but half of them belonged to the Ethiopian zone, in Africa. The Israelite diet in most places included fish. And the primary sources of fish were the Sea of Galilee and the Jordan River.

"Jesus ate broiled fish" reports St. Mark but we don't really know which species he was eating. What we do know is that Capernaum, the city of Jesus, was on the shore of the Sea of Galilee. We also know that most likely Jesus in his teens and twenties spent some time in Decapolis, a zone of Greek cities on the other side of the Sea of Galilee. Therefore, we can suggest that Jesus was not only a cook, a carpenter, a mason or bricklayer, a peasant, but also a fisherman.

"Jesus ate broiled fish" then not only tells us about the basic Israelite diet but also about Jesus' love for the sea as a fisherman.

Crucians know through experience the sea as the preserver of life. So many goodies traveled by sea, but it has a seamy side too. With the "discovery" of the New World, the commercial center moved from the Mediterranean Sea, or Roman Lake to the Caribbean Sea or "The USA Lake". The sea brought liquor, weapons, illness. The sea took our wealth, our labor, our raw materials, our history, our sense of dignity.

In Conclusion:

The sea has to do with the preservation of life, thus we have to raise our voices against people or countries who destroy it.

Last Thursday we witnessed the Vieques tragedy. More than 140 peace-makers were arrested for trying to prevent that Island from being bombarded again. The air, earth and sea military practices have deposited explosive bombs in the bottom of the sea and have contaminated the waters with radiation and other chemicals. And according to the news, in a couple of weeks the practices will continue.

One fisherman from Vieques told us that after the bombarding for 5 to 6 days in a row, he had to wait weeks in order to be able to get fish. In other words, if Jesus had visited them in the post-bombing season, Jesus wouldn't have been able to "eat broiled fish."

Fishermen from Vieques transported the peace-makers; but now that they are expelled, the same fishermen have been warned not to

35

transport them anymore; otherwise their boats will be confiscated, and they will have to pay the consequences.

During the 17th century the Danes called this 21 X 4 miles Island *Krabben Eiland*. In the mainland people think that nobody lives there, but Vieques has been inhabited for at least 4,000 years. Currently there are like 10,000 Viequenses living in St. Croix and approximately the same living in the "Isla Nena," as Puertorricans lovingly called it. No wonder the extremely skillful singer, composer and guitar player, José Feliciano sings: "Free Vieques, Free, Now" in reggae style.

This is the Bible message for today in Mark 1.17, Jesus the fisherman from Galilee is telling all of us: "Come with me, and I will teach you to become fishers of men and women."

Our world needs fishermen and fisherwomen who love and take care of the sea like the brave "Bomba" Allick Captain. Let's raise our voices in order to save the Vieques Sea. Let us never forget Pastor Niemoller's warning and raise our voices before it is too late.

36

9
BLESSED ARE THE HUNGRY
Luke 6.17-26

Africans brought many seeds to the New World, in order to feed people, in order to fit a basic need. What our brothers and sisters did —in a very clever way— was to hide seeds in their curly hair. That was how many goodies traveled from Africa to America.

The message for this morning has to do with food: "Blessed are the hungry", meaning: "God suffers in each person who goes hungry."

Paul in criticizing the Corinthians (1 Cor 15.32) quotes the saying: "Let us eat and drink, for tomorrow we will die", but our insensitive society changed it into: "Let us eat and drink, for tomorrow we will diet!"

The gospel tells us about a compassionate God, who cares for the people who suffer hunger, who suffer poverty, who weep. The beatitudes talk about God as the One who is moved to pity in every people that suffers due to the lack of the essential elements for living.

The Scripture shows us:

I. A Compassionate God

Compassion (*esplagjnizomai*, verb, and *esplagjnon*, noun) comes from womb, guts, intestines, heart, that is, the deepest emotions. Compassion points toward tenderness, nourishing, embracing, generating life. In short, compassion has to do with a warm and safe place. It is a visceral reaction, that makes us be on the side of the suffering people: those who are hungry, who weep, who can't go to court because they can't afford to pay a lawyer.

It is not by accident that the Eucharist was explained in the early Church with mother's milk, because in the same way we take our own mother's energy and vitality, Jesus himself is nourishing us out of his own body and blood with unlimited compassion.

Mother pelican, one of the main symbols of self-sacrifice throughout the ages in Christian art ilustrates this point well. We have seen many pelicans in our Caribbean islands but chances are that we haven't given a thought to them. Actually this water bird has the bad reputation of eating what belongs to the fisher people. Nevertheless, pelicans have been compared to Jesus, especially due to their red-end beak. Once upon a time there was a mother pelican who wasn't able to find any food for her brood. What she did was to immediately peak her own chest and to nourish her brood with her own blood! The Early Christian Church saw in that legend what Jesus Christ did for us, and what we, Christians, should do for our neighbors.

Our God is a God who is concerned with the basic needs of his creatures: the right to eat. Our world, on the contrary, is concerned with secondary needs. Take for example St. Valentine's Day. Egypt and Colombia, instead of producing food for the hungry, are forced to plant flowers. Colombia alone produces 148,000 tons of flowers each year! In this season of St. Valentine's Day, there are 50 Colombian airplanes transporting flowers everyday! Two out of three roses USA people will get this coming Wednesday will be from Colombia. 9 and a half out of every 10 carnations USA people will get this coming Wednesday will be from Colombia. Colombia cultivates more than 50 varieties of flowers. 83% of the Colombian flowers go to USA and Europe, including Holland, the big producer of flowers, too. Colombia, like many other Caribbean countries, is a high producer of coffee, but, strickly speaking, coffee won't solve the problem of hunger.

"Blessed are you poor, you that hunger now, you that weep now, you that are rejected and insulted." The beatitudes tell us about the

38

impossibility of loving God as God, but of loving God as he shows Godself to us, hidden in the suffering people: "I was hungry and you fed me, thirsty and you gave me a drink." (Mt 25)

The Scriptures show us:

II. A God Who Eats!

May we never forget that Christianity promotes a profound spirituality but, alongside, preaches an extremely materialistic program of action, like taking care of the hungry people.

We live in a cruel world. 35,000 children die every day in the world due to hunger and avoidable illness. In many countries like Sri Lanka or Haiti, children are born with 25 years less of life expectancy. In many countries like India, and the Dominican Republic, some people can only afford one meal a day! In many countries like Haiti, the salary per year is $250.00, less than a dollar per day! In other words, in many countries, there is a waste of food, whereas in other countries billions of people just can't eat! A USA citizen is worth 50 Haitian citizens!

Before Spaniards arrived on our Caribbean Sea, they called Christian Jews *marranos* or "pigs" because Jews who were forced to convert to Christianity had to eat pork in order to prove that their conversion was sincere, since Jews, like Jesus, don't eat pork never, ever. Ludwig Feuerbach, a Lutheran theologian said, "One is what one eats." Therefore, by eating pork the message Jewish-Christians were sending was that they really had changed religion! But St. Luke questions us today, what about if there's nothing to eat? That means that a principal source of human suffering in the modern world is still —as it has for so long been— hunger.

On the one hand, some people are so concerned about losing weight: half of USA people and 90 % of USA women -are said to be on diets at any one time. On the other hand, billions of people don't have the sacred right to eat enough. If on the one hand, USA

39

people's renowned sweet tooth focuse on dessert as the high point of the meal, on the other side, billions of people don't have the sacred right to eat the minimum. If on the one hand, USA people eat out at even higher levels of frequency, nearly one-half of the money spent on food is spent on eating out. On the other hand, billions of people don't have the sacred right to eat even at home.

Our God is a God who eats at an open table where everybody will be satisfied! Our sinful world is the opposite. In poor countries 840 million people are hungry. 200 million young children under 5 years old are undernourished. You may argue, poverty and hunger are due to wars, external debt, but also due to natural disasters. But the main cause of poverty and hunger is due to the lack of democracy in the distribution of bread.

Let me put it straight:

In this month of February, month of African-American heritage, let us keep in mind the following:

Five centuries ago the European colonial powers divided the Caribbean Islands among themselves. A century ago, in the city of Berlin, Germany, the European colonial powers divided the African Continent among themselves. In 1997, in Denver, the seven mighty countries reached an agreement of continuing to exploit the African continent. Meaning that, whereas in the northern countries there is abundant food, in Africa's subsahara, famine is the main problem. But the God of the beatitudes has sided with the poor and hungry!

Slaves commonly died of hunger, and a prime reason for marronnage -runing away- was hunger. In Jamaica before emancipation, rats were a common article of commerce. Jesus Christ as a compassionate God, by being poor himself, lived in solidarity with the poor and the hungry.

Today food travels long distances and very fast. We know how the "chiquita" banana empire is currently fighting with the European market in order to sell their products. However, in many cases the products which travel long distances don't fit basic needs but just wants and whims, like Colombian coffee and flowers! Quite different from the past. Africans brought many seeds to the New World, in order to feed people, in order to fit a basic need. What our brothers and sisters did —in a very clever way— was to hide seeds in their curly hair. That was how many goodies traveled from Africa to America.

Today we thank Africa for feeding the entire world with watermelon, ñame, malangas, gandul, bananas the-world's-most-eaten-fruit, etcetera.

The image of God we get from all of this is the one of God setting the table and sharing food with everybody and everywhere. This is the message of the gospel for this morning: "Blessed are the hungry", meaning: "God suffers in each person who goes hungry."

41

10
LET´S TALK TURKEY!
Luke 14.15-24

I hope this meditation will be a fingerlicking one. This coming Thursday 240 million people will eat the same menu, the same Turkey Day! And the party will continue on Friday with Napoleon's Day. You may ask why Friday after thanksgiving is Napoleon's day?, well, it is because on that day you take the "bone apart"!

We already know that the gospels are the stories of Jesus' tables, and that Jesus was killed because of the way he ate.[9] The story of this morning confirms that truth.

Jesus has dinner ready and an empty room, that's not very nice! The unworthy guests are not the Israelites who didn't welcome the prophets. The unworthy guests are the church leaders whose farms, business, and other concerns were more important than the Kingdom of God. Therefore, the new honored guests are "anyone off the street", the poor, the crippled, the blind, the lame, the country side people. This is an equal opportunity table. This is Jesus´ democratic table as the foretaste of the non-segregated Kingdom of God.

Eucharist is a Greek word meaning thanksgiving, and it invites us to have an open comensality, an egalitarian access to the table like in this parable. In order to reach this equal opportunity table, we have to ask 5 questions: When you can eat. How long it takes you to eat. Where you eat. What you eat. And with whom you eat.

In this parable Jesus could have given the poor some food to go, or could have invited them into the kitchen, or brought them into the living room with the whole family, or could have told them to come on Saturday night to meet the family's friends. Because there are different levels of sharing our tables, like in the working world: A cocktail party in the office for all the employees is not the same as a restaurant Lunch for all the middle managers, and it is not the same as a private dinner party for the vice-presidents in the president's home.[10]

Anyhow, please let me focus our attention on only one aspect of the table, that is, about What you eat, and especially related with food Jesus didn't eat, because America wasn't known in his time. These goodies are the basics for thanksgiving:

I. Turkey

Its native name is *huexolotl* or guajolote. Indians domesticated them since 2000 years ago. Spaniards rebaptized it as *pavo*, because they believed that it was related with the Asian "pavo real" (peacock), but they are not related at all. In 1523 *pavos* were introduced to Europe by the Spaniard Gonzalo Fernandez de Oviedo. In England it became a favorite dish for special occasions and they rebaptized it as turkey, because they thought it originated in Turkey.

La Grange State, State Prosperity and the country side of St. Croix had an excelent reputation for growing yummy turkeys!

II. Green Pepper

Spaniards found America in their attempt to reach India in order to trade plants and animals. Spaniards were dying for spices to season their food. Just imagine eating boiled rabbits without any kind of sauce! The only spice they found was chili, the principal sauce for all the dishes. In USA Virgin Islands you have your own: "Jumbie Pepper Bush." Spaniards rebaptized chili as hot peppers, which don't have to do at all with peppers!

From such misname followed other mistakes like associating chili with "Dr. Pepper" or for shorter "Pep-si" sodas! Eventually Italians changed the hot, hot flavor to a sweet one. Now Euroamericans are able to put green sweet pepper in their stuffing for the turkey!

43

III. Tomato

Its Indian name is *xitomatl* meaning belly bottom because it is similar to that part of our bodies. It took a while for Europeans to accept tomatoes. At first they feared they were poisonous and their leaves smelled too strong for their taste. Besides that, Europeans rejected tomatoes and other American goodies because they weren't mentioned in the Bible!

Europeans didn't know what to do: when the tomato was green, it was uneatable. When it was red, it smelled like it were spoiled. When boiled or fried it got into pieces. As time went by, Italy and Spain built their cuisines on the delicacy of native American tomatoes.

In the 20th century USA made juice out of tomato and also mixed it up with spirits, like the "bloody Mary." For Thanksgiving tomato is present in the stuffing, too.

IV. Corn

Centéotl, corn Goddess is the divinity who fights hunger. Its original name of corn is *Tlaolli,* then it was changed to Haitian *Mahis.* When the Spaniards arrived in America the first thing they learned from the Indians was to make "pop corn." There are more than 60 varieties of corn. It has been domesticated for at least 7500 years. The Portuguese took it to Africa where it has been basic for their diet, whereas in Europe it has been used to feed the animals. They don't eat corn, not even in the form of "corn flakes."

What the potato did for the European population, corn did for European animals: it simply saved them from starvation.

Centuries before the invention of "Tang" to please the astronauts with "fresh orange juice," American Indians developed the techniques to preserve peppers, meat, potatoes... by drying and grinding them. Corn powder or *pinolli*, then facilitated people to move around in big distances. "Chicha" or corn beer is another ancient creation but "that's another enchilada!"

Italians rebaptized corn as "grain of Turkey" following that

44

obsession with Turkey! A Thanksgiving meal includes cornbread stuffing, corn on the cob, and corn as a decoration!

V. Potato

We are used to hearing "Irish potato" or "French fries" but potato is from America. Indians of the Andes before Columbus' arrival cultivated around 3,000 varieties of potatoes. Peruvians have planted this root for more than 4,000 years.[11]

In Spanish we keep the Peruvian name *papa*. The English word *potato* comes from the Spaniards *patata*, which originally was the Taino Indian's *batata*, which refered to sweet potato. When the British met the "real" potato they had to distinguish between "sweet potato" and "common potato" in spite of the fact that both tubers are not related at all![12]

In Saint Thomas there is a bench on a beautiful hill facing the sea where history tells us Francis Drake the fearful pirate sat down." He never made it to Puerto Rico but he sent enough gold to England that the monarchy declared him an honorable person. In Offenburg, Germany, there is a monument to Sir Francis Drake, who holds a potato in his hand, and there is a plaque saying: "To Sir Francis Drake who introduced the potato to Europe in 1586. In the name of millions of peasants who bless his eternal memory."[13]

Europeans considered potato a source of leprosy due to its misshapen and ugly form. The prestigious French Encyclopédie (1765) of Denis Diderot blamed the potato for causing excess flatulence.[14] That "couch potato" of Diderot didn't do his homework.

In Russia they didn't like the dirty root. They declared potato a botanical monstrosity for not being listed in the Bible.[15] Little did they know that vodka was to be make out of potatoes!

45

VI. Beans

Its original name is *Ayacotl* or *etl*. Spaniards found a similitude with the Roman fava, so they rebaptized it as fesoles and from there, comes the Spanish frijoles.

The British found a similitude with the insect called *bean weevi* and from there, comes the name beans.

VII. Pumpkin

Ayotl is its real name, and it has been eaten for approximately 9,500 years. Italians re-called it "Zucco of Syria"and from there comes zucchini. When the Muslims tasted pumpkins, they applied to it their tradition of stuffing vegetables. Indians made soup, zucchini flower tacos, medicine, and salads out of pumpkins. The English language keeps the Massachusetts Indian name *askootasquash*. For thanksgiving now they are used as decorations and of course, as a delicious pumpkin pie dessert!

VIII. Chocolate

Xocolatl is its name. Before it became the "Swiss chocolate" of the "Viennese cafeteria", it was too bitter for most European tastes because it was drunk in the form of Cacao, a word later corrupted to cocoa. Currently there's a gluttony for chocolate in USA, England, France, Holland, West Germany, etc. You may very well invite chocolate to your turkey day!

Other trimmings include cranberry sauce from the 47 types of berries Indians cultivated. Each of those types had variations, like the 20 varieties of blue berries, or the popular cherrie: "violence is American as cherrie pie." (Rap Brown) You may close your meal with Vanilla ice cream.

Eucharist is a Greek word meaning thanksgiving and invites us to have an open comensality, an egalitarian access to the table, like in this parable. Crucians used to celebrate an open Thanksgiving day in St. Patrick's school yard and in St. Gerard's Hall. Crucians used to say "St. Patrick's was the beat". There was lots of music of Archie and Wesley Thomas' Orchestra. As Cherra Heyliger tells s, the dance time was with Skipio and Edwin Thomas and the Vibratones.

The Kingdom of God is precisely that, an open comensality, where there is room for everybody!

46

BREAD: JESUS' POLITICAL PROGRAM
John 6. 24-35

Jesus Christ, as we know, was killed for the way he ate.[16] It's not for nothing that the Gospels are concerned especially with eating, with bread, with the table, with banquets. Therefore, we should not be surprised to find this theme again on this eighth Sunday after Pentecost. When Jesus states: "I am the bread of life" he not only shares the bread but gives of himself, and as a consequence, he is also signing his death sentence. Today bread is a mortal weapon that people and hoarding countries use to keep two thirds of the world population hungry.

The day after the feeding of a multitude of more than 5000 people, some of them reached Jesus on the other side of the sea of Galilee with the hidden intention of continuing to be fed by Jesus. But he does not fall into the trap of the tricky question: "Master, when did you arrive here?" He simply answered them: I assure you that you seek me because you ate your fill, and not because you have understood the signs of the Kingdom of God."

Allow me to linger on only two aspects of this Kingdom of God of which we currently have also not understood or do not wish to understand: The Kingdom of God as a table in solidarity and as an open table.

I. The Kingdom of God as a Table of Solidarity

What happened the day before this encounter was not the miracle of the multiplication of bread and fish, as we have so conveniently tended to understand it. NO! What really happened was the outpouring of human solidarity. The little boy set the example when he shared his two loaves of bread and two fish. After him there were other followers of Jesus, so that everyone ate their full. But there were always among the multitude selfish ones who instead of sharing their fish sandwiches, preferred to selfishly get their fill. Their selfishness prevented them from seeing the novelty of Jesus Christ's table, where bread is to be shared and not kept back.

Secondly:

II. The Kingdom of God as an Inclusive Table

As we recall, the table reflects and reinforces better than any other piece of furniture in our homes, the type of society we live in. Therefore, in order to know our social order better, it is helpful to ask ourselves: what, where, when, and with whom do we eat?

When we cross the barrier of another culture, the two most difficult obstacles to be overcome are the language and the food, although it is changing due to the Macdonaldization of food. However, when a high priest of the Ethiopian Jews that returned to the state of Israel was interviewed, he was asked how they were able to maintain their identity from their origin with the Queen of Sheba and King Solomon until presently, approximately some 2,900 years. The priest answered: We have protected our identity because "we have never eaten with someone that was not from our own group."[17] In Jesus' Jewish culture, not only was it prohibited to marry pagans, but also condemned to eat with gentiles. But Jesus' table is open: there is no restriction of persons.

In Jesus' society slaves had to eat standing up, while the free people lay on the floor on mats and reclined to eat with the fingers of one hand. This implied that someone had to serve them. There were not only places of honor but also food and drink of honor. The quality of wine and food depended on the rank of the guest. But

48

Jesus' table is open: "Let all people sit down" said Jesus, and may all be served equally. That was a disrupting action. And at the Last Supper, He Himself served the table.

Jesus repudiated the oppressive laws of purity and politeness at the table. Jesus had to pay with his death on the cross for this political program proposed at his inclusive table.

The invention of silverware in the 15th century was a way of having a private plate and no longer eating from a common or community pot. It also intended to create distance from the food, and not to touch it with the fingers. The prohibition of putting the elbows on the table had to do with the right of not invading the others' territory. The table then is a place where we can observe the body language of distance and coldness or the body language of touching and closeness, as table manners has been elaborated for centuries: "At table, wait to be served, do not be greedy, do not stretch out your hands toward the serving dish, do not lick your lips, do not open your mouth too wide, do not speak before you have emptied it. Keep your elbows down, do not dip your bread in your wine, do not pick your teeth with a knife, do not dry off your sweat with your napkin —in short do not do any of those things that lords are allowed to do, as if they were the lords of the earth."[18]

Let me piggyback to the main points:

Jesus' political program: "I am the bread of life" has to do with a model of an inclusive and solidary society.

In the late 19th century New York things hadn't changed: "In blue-collar restaurants, thousands of people eat standing up, with their hats on, all in a line, like horses in a stable."[19]

As a Lutheran Caribbean church we must continue to reinforce our identity as an open and solidary table. Thanks be to God that in our sanctuaries the table is central, and thanks be to God that in our worship, the table is also central. But we must be careful not to spiritualize bread, following some liturgies that speak of the Eucharistic bread as "bread of angels." The table in our parishes, as well as the table in our homes must be open and solidary tables in the midst of a selfish and excluding society such as ours.

Ponce de León, the conqueror of Puerto Rico, used to have his dogs sit at the table. Today things haven't changed. There are Caribbean countries, vegetarian not by choice, that have never tasted the fish they catch and send to the northern countries to serve as food for their dogs and cats. In 1997 alone, the USA and Europe spent 17 billion dollars in food for pets![20]

The Haitians that work in the bateys in the Dominican Republic have only one meal a day, the rest of the day they drink sugar cane juice. In Sri Lanka there are those who eat rotten wood with honey in order to get their vitamin B. In some countries in the south we have to eat dirt in order to supply some minerals for our bodies.

On the other hand, we have closed tables of societies so concerned with losing weight, with diets, with the obsessive counting of calories taken each hour. Societies of "we´re going dutch" each one with their own food, with selfish and excluding tables.

Jesus is very clear in his position: he is not in a campaign in search for votes, for admirers or flatterers that sell themselves for a plate of lentils. Jesus is not afraid of scaring off the clients. He confronted His own disciples by asking them: "Do you want to leave me too?" (John 6.67) Our liberator Jesus Christ asks us to be disciples in the task of building a society of solidary and inclusive tables with the bread of life! Amen.

50

12
THE RIGHT TO EAT!
Matthew. 20. 1-16

Don Ché David, a Puertorrican Lutheran theologian and pastor told me the other day that a "hillbilly" (a jibarito) quoted St. Paul's text as "the laborer deserves a double salary!" (1 Tim 5.18)

Our text for today also talks about laborers and wages. The parable of the laborers in the vineyard is a lesson on the values of justice of the Kingdom of God. This parable tells us above all of the right to work or to say the same, the right to eat, or the right to live.

Unfortunately, many other interpretations have remained, which obscures the meaning of the laborers in the vineyard. Allow me to mention some examples:

I. The Interpretation of Efficiency

The rabbis used to tell a parable, according to that: "a king had many laborers, but one was an unusually good worker. The king permitted him to work for 2 hours and then let him off, and when he gave him the same pay as the others, his answer to the objectors was 'this man has done more in 2 hours than you have done in the entire day.'"

According to that, the skillful workers have the right to work less because they are more efficient.

II. The Interpretation of Unselfishness

The rabbis also like to reject the work that is done because of rewards and not because of the love of God.

They like to mention: "do not be like slaves who serve the master for the sake of reward, but be like slaves who serve the master not for the sake of reward and let the fear of heaven be upon you." (Aboth, 1:3)

The conclusion from this interpretation is that the laborers that work 12 hours should not complain about receiving the same wage of the laborers that only worked one hour, because we should be unselfish, and our work must please God and not our human bosses.

III. The Interpretation of the Spiritual Meaning

Some Christians have interpreted the parable of the laborers in the vineyard, by explaining that the landowner is God, the vineyard is Israel, and the payment the last judgement. This is the interpretation of the artist that designed our buletin.

Patriarchs and prophets worked a 12 hour journey whereas the disciples only worked one hour, or if you prefer: Jews worked 12 hours and we pagans only one, but all of us receive the same salvation. It is not by merit but by grace alone. Some people converted to Jesus Christ a long time ago but they and the latecomers will receive the same salvation.

IV. The Interpretation of Women's Rights

Some Christian women have seen in the parable of the laborers in the vineyard a denunciation of the low and unequal labor wages they get.

Women workers know that they have access only to 30% of the jobs. That they perform 60% of the work all over the world. That they earn only 10% of the salary and the other 90% are for men.

This interpretation, like some of the others, has some ingredients of truth, but allow me to mention a fifth interpretation:

V. The Right to Eat

This is the story of a landowner who hired workers at 6, 9, and

52

12 am, and at 3 and 5 pm. The ones that were able to work 12 hours were so lucky. They started their labor day from 6 am to 6 pm, or as our African-american ancestors used to say: "from can't to can't", namely, "from I can't see in the morning to I can't see in the evening." These fortunate 12-hour journey laborers received their daily wage of one denarius or one dracma, which was the normal day's pay for manual workers, and which barely covered their basic needs.

The laborers that were hired at the eleventh hour, namely, at 5 pm or at one hour before sundown, represent not the lazy people but the idle people that want to work but were not able to find a job. The landowner gave them also a full day's pay because he knew that "if they went home with wages for only a single hour, their families could not be fed" (J. Jeremías). The landowner didn't know our hillbilly friend, otherwise he would have given the laborers "a double salary".

In other words, the laborers in the vineyard parable has to do with the right to work, or to say the same, the right to eat that we Lutherans remember every Sunday at Jesus Christ's Table.

The 4th commandment that tells us about the resting day is the same commandment that reminded us about the right to work 6 full days, because the Bible knows that without work there is no bread on our tables and therefore there is no life.

The world economy is now divided between the included and the excluded people. We are facing the 21st century with millions of women and men, that are not able to work not even one hour a day. They are completely excluded. The shame of our new millenium are the hundreds of countries that are used for cheap labor and unfair wages: In Haiti for instance, there are companies with 10 hour schedules, and only allow their workers to go to the bathroom twice a day, and they give them 10 minutes to eat and earn one dollar a day.

Our friend the hillbilly that used to say: "the laborer deserves a

53

double salary" can very well say today: "the laborers deserve 10 salaries" in order to put bread on their tables.

The liberating news of this parable is that God, and the Christian church have taken the side of the last, of the unemployed, of the excluded countries, of the rejected human beings. God is summoning us this morning to hold hands specially with the most unfortunate idle people in order to promote the right to work, the right to eat, the right to live!

54

13
NEITHER GREATNESS, NOR SERVITUDE
Mark 9.30-37

The Aminas tribe which was brought from Africa to the West Indies in order to labor in the plantations, was one of the bravest in seeking liberation from bondage. From the very beginning they rejected servitude and preferred to commit suicide before being enslaved. During the freedom fight of St. John in 1733-34, the Aminas made suicide more acceptable than the chains of servitude. The Aminas was a very religious tribe which used to pray at all times: at sunset, at sunrise, upon eating and drinking, when taking to the field, etc. Singing was in the Aminas´ blood even in the midst of the uprising. The doctrine of "migrations of souls", was a source of hope. According to them, when one dies the soul re-incarnates in another body in Guinea, their motherland. The Aminas planned massive suicide as a mean of repudiating servitude and returning to Africa to start a life of plenty. Aminas went as far as killing their children before commiting suicide, in order for everybody to be reincarnated in a new land far away from the West Indies' inhuman physical bondage[21].

Now, the three introductory lines for today's Gospel states: "The antidote to such a concern for greatness is servanthood." But these three lines are not part of the biblical text, in fact, these three lines contradict the very core of the gospel text.

What the gospel for this morning is telling us is that Jesus requires from us "neither greatness, nor servitude but discipleship."

I. Jesus Calls Us Neither to Greatness, nor to Servitude.
People who look for greatness have changed the meaning of

servanthood to servitude. Some apostles went pursuing greatness by means of subjugating the others to servitude like their perverse world of 2,000 years ago. 500 years ago some countries started dominating other countries in a big scale and transforming them into servitude countries. In our evil societies all over the world men are encouraged to dominate women and to consider women as servitude. Poor married women are not only servants, but "servants of servants", that is, servants of their husbands who they themselves are servants. Poor women have a double and some times a multiple servitude!

In the church we have deacons and deaconesses, these are two Greek words: dia and konos, which mean, through and dust. The deacons were the people in charge of taking the camels through the desert, therefore their feet were dusty because of that dirty job. The Christian church has been very picky in sharing power, with the people; however, on matters of service, the Christian church has been very sharing. The disciples were arguing for the positions of power but not for the positions of service. The issue is that, in society and unfortunately in the Christian church too, we have confused servanthood with servitude. In fact, when the church calls to service it is really calling to servitude, but Jesus is neither calling us to greatness and power nor to servitude.

II. Jesus Calls Us to Discipleship

All Christians should follow Jesus neither with a spirit of greatness, nor with a spirit of servitude.

The problem is that, for ages, some Christians have cultivated a spirit of greatness and have chosen other people to cultivate a spirit of servitude. Namely, some people are being served and some people have served more than others. Some countries have been served and some countries have been the permanent servers. In Mexico the Roman Catholic priest Las Casas defended the Indians from servitude but he didn't defend the African-mexicans. Right now in the political campaigns politicians are addressing the issue of the immigrants, or the people condemned to permanent servitude. Politicians don't want to liberate them, what they want is the vote of the people as they show concern for servitude.

"Neither greatness, nor servitude, but discipleship" is related with the issue of power. It has to do with the domination/subordination relationship. Let's take a look in our own families, who is in charge? Who holds power and greatness?

Our evil world is organized in terms that some people are to enjoy greatness and others suffer servitude. The Olympic games are taking place in Australia but where are the indigenous Australians? Native Australians are condemned to servitude and British-Australians are the ones to pursue greatness. How is it that usually the same countries are the gold medal winners? Why have some people been predestined to play the role of servitude and others the role of greatness? The motto of the YMCA (Young Men's Christian Association) was "we are the winning team".

A Final Word:
In Jesus Christ's open table there is no room neither for greatness nor for servitude but for discipleship; that is the lesson for all of us today.

Let me finish with two examples: The medical guidebooks of the last century recommended for the middle class adolescent girls not to do physical labor such as strenuous domestic chores. Mature middle class women were prohibited any physical activity during menstruation, and those medical books considered regular work schedules as injurious to a woman's health. But all those recomendations for middle class women didn't apply for poor women who were considered as property.[22] In the case of the poor working people their sin is not their lack of service but too much service, which is servitude.

57

The open egalitarian table of Jesus was challenged by Jim Jones, nonetheless, he is mainly remembered because of the Peoples Temple, and Jonestown over 900 revolutionary mass murder-suicide. What happened on November 18, 1978, in the Caribbean jungles of Guyana was dismissed by sensationalistic press and instant books, as a movement of brainwashed zombies led by a monster. However, a closer look shows us quite another story. Jonestown was an ideal society integrated by 75% African-Americans. It was a socialist paradise which opposed elitism, sexism, classism, ageism, and above all, racism. It was a community where two-thirds were women and 80% people of color. In 1977 Jones was a recipient of the Martin Luther King Jr. Humanitarian of the Year Award and Jonestown was praised "as a refuge for the young urban 'incorrigible'". A white survivor of the religious mass murder-suicide, Michael Prokes considered the tragedy "violence that violence had created": "When the congressional delegation of Leo Ryan arrived, the visit was perceived as a dangerous threat by an arrogant white person representing that white establishment, which pushed the Jonestown community up against the wall. The result could be perceived as a violent response to the systemic violence inherent in white institutions, the urban aparheid of American cities, the white power structure that dominates American society, the structural violence of subclassification against which the Peoples Temple had struggled throughout its history."[23]

What some disciples were pursuing was greatness, that is, to be served and to chain others into servitude. That behavior shows us the current attitude of people who don't serve at all and people who serve too much. No wonder the Aminas tribe of the West Indies preferred suicide rather than a miserable life of servitude.

Jesus Christ rejects greatness and servitude and calls us to follow him through his open and egalitarian table.

58

14
I SHALL NOT WANT
Psalm 23

In London, 1883, Abram Lyle was quietly selling "Golden Syrup," or simply put, refined molasses. Eventualy "Goldie," would get a big market and became the famous product of Tate & Lite. Abram the III was in charge of selecting a trade mark, and he used the Bible story of Samson. The can showed the lion killed by Samson, and surrounded by bees, and the quotation from Judges 14 "Out of the strong came forth sweetness." The famous green-and-gold Golden Syrup tin can shows a dead lion, the lion Samson killed, surrounded by bees; they have nested in the lion's belly and made honey. We all know that story and by now all of us realize that Samson's riddle had to do with honey; and Golden Syrup is made from sugar. Whether the motive of simple religious piety is convincing enough to account for the choice of a honey symbol to sell sugar syrup, it's up to us to decide. But what is important here is to notice the birth of a new way for the honest description of one's product. The Bible was used to sell products even by misquoting it, even not telling the truth. Since then we are encouraged to buy honey but, under an appearance of biblical piety they are selling us sugar.[24]

Psalm 23 the favorite psalm of Christians, has been used for funeral services, for comforting burdened people. It was sung at a meal sponsored by a worshiper as part of his or her thanksgiving. The early church sang this psalm once the baptized person emerged from the font and was ready to take the Eucharist. Today let us meditate on Psalm 23 and the daily activities of eating, drinking and having protection in a shelter. This Psalm has to do with the essentials of life v. 1, "I shall not want" or "I have everything I need."

I. God Prepares the Table Before Us. 5a.

God makes us lie down in green pastures" means that God is interested in feeding us. God is placing "tablecloths," "table music," "tableware," lighting the candles, adding flowers, refreshing our heads with oil and perfume. God is giving us real food within a festive environment because all God's creatures are worthy of having access to fancy tables. The first thing Jesus did for the people he fed was to invite them to sit (John 6.10). That was a disrupting action because poor people were forbidden to sit while eating. Young children observe if mom eats together with the family or if she eats standing up. Right now in many places workers are allowed to take only 10 minutes for lunch!

II. God Fills Our Cups to the Brim. 5c.

According to Is 21.14 water is the essential drink, but our gracious host walks the second mile; he is offering us a small luxury, that is, wine. In Judges 19.4 wine is associated with honoring somebody and with a festive time. Every time the Bible says they ate and drank, it refers to drinking wine because of a special occasion.

Furthermore, our psalm says our cups overflow. God is serving us with great generosity, and not in ordinary glasses but in wine cups. Cups that were exclusive for the kings and their powerful families around are now accessible to us.

60

III. God is Sheltering Us. 6b.

Since the stone age, our ancestors knew about the right to own a cavern. This basic need is also portrayed in this Psalm. "I shall dwell in the house of YHVH" or "your house will be my home as long as I live." Jesus Christ, our Savior who didn't have a place to lie his head knows what we're talking about. Jesus lived his last years in Capernaum with the extended family of Peter, in a borrowed corner. Therefore God is specially sensitive towards the basic human need of having a shelter.

Allow Me to go Back to the Golden Syrup Business:

Our Psalm states: God is my shepherd who provides me food, drink and shelter, so "I shall lack nothing," "I have everything I need," or "I shall not want." Advertising, on the other hand, associates products with what are otherwise desirable thoughts, admirable persons, good works, good health, divine causes, humanitarian actions. However, like in the case of Samson's story, advertising doesn't tell us the truth.

In the same way that in 1883 we got sugar instead of honey, our evil society keeps selling us not only what we don't want but what we don't need. "I shall not want" says our psalm. "You need this, and this, and this, says our perverted world." Our consumer oriented society is driven by greed rather than need and in doing so is oriented towards profit and not towards satisfying real needs like food, drink, and housing.

We are living in a world of plenty but where there are millions of people starving. What former generations considered incredible luxuries, today we have been forced to believe that they are necessities. We haven't learned the meaning of "I shall not want." The advertisement mentioned announced honey and gave us sugar; in our case we're bombarded by hundreds of messages selling us things we really don't need. They've created imaginary needs instead of considering basic necessities because we're not alert and we forget that God is our shepherd and we "shall not want." Some weeks ago an article of "St. Croix's Avis" was denouncing that, while Crucian merchants were going to bankruptcy, big fishes are profiting here.

Currently hundreds of countries spend less than 10% of their budget on agriculture, France's budget is 5%, while 800 billion dollars are spent in the military business in the world.

Today we ask for bread and we receive a weapon. Little wonder tragedies happen like in Littleton, Colorado and its school violence. In the USA alone there are 230 million weapons. Our sister Island of Vieques also suffered the mortal bombing last week. Kosovo is but another example of how we prefer to change bread, drink and shelter into destruction and death.

Let's get together around Jesus Christ's communion table, and let us be as generous as him, by sharing our food, our drink and our homes with the people in need, in order for them to be able to say: "I shall not want." As Isaiah 2.4 proposes, "God will settle disputes among great nations. They will hammer their swords into plows and their spears into pruning knives. Nations will never again go to war, never prepare for battle again." Let our countries change their weapons into instruments to cultivate the land in order for the poor countries to be able to say: "I shall not want."

62

15
PIE, PIE IN THE SKY, BY AND BY!
John 6. 35,41-51

The Christian church not only during the time of slavery but in all ages, has had the temptation of spiritualizing the Biblical message and emptying the material content of the tidings of great joy of Jesus Christ. Passages like the one for this morning of Jn 6.35 have been interpreted in a wrong way. "Whoever comes to me will never be hungry" seems to talk about Jesus being exclusively interested in spiritual hunger, but nothing further from the truth!

John 6.35 is the continuation of the controversy of Capernaum we have been following for a couple of Sundays. John is telling us that the bread of life liberates us from death and that what gives us life is the flesh of Jesus, his body that will endure death on the cross. But! Let us never forget the truth, that Jesus shows himself as the bread of our souls only after feeding the multitude of 5,000 people. Jesus is very much interested in the material bread and in the spiritual bread as well.

The spiritual hunger of John 6.35 reminds us of Deut 8.3: "human beings don't live on bread alone." But! Let us never forget the truth that Moses shows God as the bread of our souls only after feeding the multitude of thousands with the mana of the desert. Moses is very much interested in the material mana and in the spiritual bread as well.

The "Pie, pie in the sky, by and by!" was the way sinful Christians denied the material bread and only preached the spiritual bread. Pie, pie in the sky, by and by! is the way the State has understood the church ministry of dealing exclusively with the souls of the people and if the church dared to stand on the side of the physically hungry people, the State would get antsy.

In fact, Desmond Tutu, the African Anglican bishop calls Christianity the most materialistic religion! The Russian Nicolas Berdiaef raised his voice: "If I´m talking about bread for my neighbor, that´s a spiritual matter, if I´m talking about bread for myself, that´s a material matter." The Brazilian Dom Helder Camara also protested: "If I give to the poor a piece of bread, they call me a saint, but if I raise the question: how is it that there are so many hungry people?, they call me a communist."

The unbelief of the leaders of the Jews is still present among us. We prefer to believe in a God who belongs to another world or who is present only in our inner hearts, or in the Eucharistic table. We, like the unbelief of the Jews, forget that Jesus is present wherever 2 or 3 persons are gathered in his name. And we also forget that Jesus is present through others, especially through the most needy. (Mt 25)

The Christian church has spent a lot of time and resources arguing about her mission: Are we called to evangelize and save souls? or it is our mission to feed the physically hungry? John is direct in his answer: Feed the physically hungry and feed the spiritually hungry! And I would add, let's do it in this order: first the material bread, then the spiritual bread! Allow me to mention one example: I remember a very pious Christian sister who got sick and was hospitalized. She just lost all her physical energy and vitality. When a physician examined her, she confessed to him: listen, doctor, my heart is in trouble because I just can't pray to my Savior! The physician told her: "don't worry at all, your body is very, very weak, it is natural not to be able to pray. When you get well your desire to pray will come back, please, don't worry." Wow! Many of us Christians and pastors have to learn from this physician that without a healthy body we can't have a healthy spirit!

64

For our liberator Jesus Christ both material and spiritual bread are important, both go hand and glove! Jesus repudiated the saying "Pie, pie in the sky, by and by!

Jesus fed the multitude of the 5,000 people regardless of their acceptance of the spiritual bread. Jesus didn't say: "if you follow me, then I'll give you this or that." Jesus says: "Whoever comes to me will never be hungry." He says whoever, he doesn't say "you have to come to me."

Pie, pie in the sky, by and by was a misunderstanding of Christianity which promotes pie in the sky but first, pie, pie on the earth, come and come!

16
SAINT LAZARUS' DAY AND THE PHYSICALLY CHALLENGED
Luke 16. 19-31

Since the Spaniard's colonial days, our sister island of Cuba celebrates Saint Lazarus' Day on December 16-17. Saint Lazarus, a national saint is portrayed with rags, with crutches and with dogs licking his open sores. Lazarus, the hungry person with disabilities, different from ours, is the same one our lectionary is honoring this morning.

On their knees, with dragging feet, shoeless, exhausted, a myriad of pilgrims arrive at "El Rincón," (The Corner) Catholic Church, some 9.5 miles away from Habana.

Lazarus, the cripple loiterer is the compassionate New Testament person who receives and helps the physically and mentally challenged folks, the sick, the lepers, the poorest of the poor, the have-nots, the dregs of society. The poorly dressed crowd visit Saint Lazarus to thank him for his help since he himself knew in his own flesh what it means to be despicable and excluded from the table.

The gospel lesson of today raises two issues: social and gastronomic criticism.

I. Social Critique
The parable of Lazarus and the rich man has been interpreted throughout history in terms of not putting our trust in someone else but Jesus; in terms of what hell looks like; in terms of how we have to learn to be good neighbors; in terms of what would be the final

destination of the Rich man's five brothers; or worst yet, in terms of "pie, pie in the sky, bye and bye": you suffer patiently here but in the "after world" you will make it! In all these interpretations, I'm afraid we have missed the main meaning: Jesus' parables are related with social criticism.

The very characters of this parable show Jesus' radical view of society. A person living in misery usually an anonymous man, has a name; the man living in luxury, usually a big fish, doesn't own a name!

The crippled beggar's name is Lazarus, a name which comes from Eleazar, like my youngest sister, meaning "God has helped." According to Jesus, God has taken the side of the physically challenged.

2,000 years ago, in Jesus' culture, the people with disabilities different from our own, were considered rejected by God. The fact that they had a physical or mental challenge was understood as a sin they or their parents had committed and God, in response, punished them with blindness, deafness, etc. Therefore, they had to struggle with their physical challenge plus their social condemnation.

Handicaped or disabled gives the idea of incomplete or abnormal people. Greeks and Romans didn't give a penny for the mentally or physically challenged persons. St. Augustine closed heaven for deaf people since, according to his reading of Romans 10.17, "faith comes by hearing, and hearing the word of God."

By the 16th century this cruel way of behaving hadn't changed. Our spiritual father Martin Luther, was of the idea that hareliped persons were the result of having intercourse with the demons! Therefore, they had to struggle with their physical challenge and their social condemnation as well.

67

Even today in the 21^{rst} century people and institutions including Christian churches are very insensitive towards the physically challenged, and we would be surprised how many of them are kept inside the closet.

Well, on the other side, we have the rich man whose name is not even mentioned by Jesus. This action was in itself very disruptive. The early tradition baptized the rich man as Neues, Phinees, Nineve, or Finaeus because it was unbearable not to mention such an important person by name! By the end of the Middle Ages the adjective "rich" or dives in Latin, was converted into a proper name: Dives. Now it was much better for some people to refer to this parable as Lazarus and Dives, being Dives the gourmet food lover, in contrast to Lazarus, the hungry cripple.

In the beginning of the 20th century there are more than a billion Lazaruses in our planet. The Caribbean and Latin America have more than 211 million poor people and 89 million of them live in misery like Lazarus. The World Bank reported that 2.4 billion Lazaruses in the world have less wealth than 385 individuals. Under the excuse of the terrorist attacks in New York and Washington, around 100, 000 people are losing their jobs in the United States and around 250,000 will be jobless throughout the world.

This parable helps us to understand that even though 92% of USA people support war, a distinction needs to be made between the wealthy family of Osama Bin Laden and millions of Lazaruses of Afghanistan, who are already suffering because of the food blockade. A few years ago the United Nations estimated that in Afghanistan there were half a million physically challenged people partially as a result of the invasions of England and Russia.

After 335 years of Lutheranism in the Virgin Islands now we have in the Rev. Margarita Martínez, not only the first female bishop but, one of the few physically challenged bishops. Being herself a physically challenged person, she can lead our Caribbean Synod in such a way that our churches may be sensitive towards the less fortunate people of society, the hungry folks and the people with disabilities different from our own, because all of us have some kind of disability.

But this parable also contains a

68

II. Gastronomic Critique

Silverware and napkins either made out of paper or of cloth are out of the picture in Jesus' culture. Besides that, rich and poor in Jesus' culture used to eat with their fingers, exactly like our African and Indian Caribbean and American cultures. By the time food arrived in their mouths, it was already tasted by their fingers. In order to clean the mouth and fingers from greasy goodies, in Mexico we do it by licking, or better yet, we still use corn tortillas, however we usually don't throw it under the table, we eat it right away, we call it "recycling!"

The sumptuous table of our parable doesn't have room for such gross table manners. Therefore, what they did was to use pieces of bread exclusively for cleaning their hands. Once they wiped their hands, they threw them under the table. The first come first serve of the dirty pieces of bread were the rich man's dogs, as we remember Jesus' conversation with the Syrophoenitian woman (Mk 7.28). The leftovers of the dogs then were thrown down to the streets and the last and least to eat the scraps were the beggars, who were also thrown out in the streets.

In other words, bread, a basic need, was corrupted into a napkin, exactly like today the fancy tables use lettuce and other basic food just for decoration, while legions of Lazaruses are begging for something to eat.

Lazarus was thrice oppressed. First as a cripple, second as a hungry person and third by being considered an unclean person because of his skin illness. No wonder the Scripture says that even the dogs licked his ulcerated sores!

69

Cuban Saint Lazarus' Day is a clear example of how the hungry and the physically challenged are desperate for bread and medicine in a country which has endured a food blockade for over 40 years. It is not by chance that Saint Lazarus is not only the Christians' champion but also the protector of the Afro-Caribbean religion of Santería. Saint Lazarus has been recreated in Babalú Ayé.

In the same Roman Catholic Church of "El Rincón" outside Habana, you may see how Christians and Santeros feed Saint Lazarus with their best food and drinks, and luxuries: "local food, rum and tobacco."

Let me repeat it:

The air we are breathing smells of war, but thank God for people like the Afro-American Barbara Lee, the congress woman for Oakland, Alameda and Berkeley, who was one out of 420 representatives of Congress who opposed going to war because it would produce who knows how many hundreds of thousands of more physically challenged and hungry, innocent children, female and male Lazaruses. Barbara Lee is able to see how the Operation "Infinite Justice" may bring "Infinite Lazaruses."

We should keep in mind Martin Luther King's warning in commenting Lazarus and Dives parable. He told us that America is going to hell too, if she fails to bridge the gulf between blacks and whites; between Northern and Southern countries.

May the living memory of Saint Lazarus, with his crutches and the dogs licking his open wounds awaken in us compassion and solidarity with the last and the least, here and now. St. Croix used to have a leper's colony by 1933 but then they were taken away to the mainland.

Lazarus, meaning "God has helped" tells us that he is not a sinner, he is clean. overty and richness are not God's will; they are the result of humankind's "infinite injustice." Lazarus has been honored by reclining his head on Abraham's bosom, the host of the banquet! (John 13.23), whereas the rich man, even after he died, keeps on arguing with arrogance.[25]

Let's see Jesus in the physically challenged and hungry people, as he tells us: "Because I was hungry and you fed me, come and have supper with me."

70

17
THE WOMAN WHO DEFEATED JESUS!
Mark 7.24-30

The way we treat dogs changes according to times. Currently, in Europe and in the USA dogs even go to school, and in Christian churches during the prayers of the people, some pray for their dogs. Some folks put their dogs first place in their wills. There's a sticker for couples that says: "we're staying together for the sake of the dogs."

Spaniards like Ponce de Leon used to sit his dogs at his table because dogs and horses were mortal weapons in their conquering of America. Dogs were very dear because they captured run-away people who were protesting for their living conditions.

In Jesus' time crucifixion was one of the supreme Roman penalties especially because of the vultures who cried above the cross and the scavenger dogs who growled beneath the dead body. To be crucified was to be "evil food for birds of prey and grim pickings for dogs."[26] It was not for nothing that *dog* was also the name Jews chose to name Gentiles.

In short, dogs were considered evil, unclean and undesirable animals (Psalm 22.16,20). We should keep this in mind when we hear Jesus calling the Syrophoenician woman a dog.

Jesus is in Gentile soil, breaking the purity norms, perhaps because he is so exhausted and does not want to mingle with anybody. But here comes a foreign woman who breaks all the rules: she is a Gentile from Canaan (Egyptian word for the Greek Phoenician) the eternal enemy of Israel. She is from another religion which the Bible calls

"Greek," but it means any other religion different from Judaism. One of her ancient gods is called Belzeebul, who Jews considered Satan. And furthermore, the Syrophoenician is a woman: how dare she approach a strange man in an unknown house? How dare she represent her daughter since that was the business of the father or any other male relative? And still more, how dare she disturb Jesus?

Well, what we expected to happen happened: Jesus was so rude and hostile in comparing her and her daughter with little dogs or puppies. We may justify Jesus' unrefined words by quoting a little bit of history in order to realize that poor Galilean peasant farmers were the ones who produced food for Canaanite wealthy cities. We may argue that Jesus was conscious of economic oppression caused by the fellows of the Syrophoenician woman. Therefore, it could very well be that, what lay behind Jesus' answer was: "Let my people eat their own crops and do not let them be taken by your folks." But, still, this Canaanite's economic exploitation doesn't satisfy Jesus' angry dismissal of the Syrophoenician woman.

And here we are with the stubborn lady, daring to argue with Jesus. Jesus, the extremely skillful man in oral combat, ended up recognizing her superiority and victory in argument. Jesus knows how to lose an argument. This woman is welcomed by Jesus for her unconventional behavior, her assertiveness, her boldness, cleverness, for her challenging customary social roles that stand in the way of helping those in need.

But, above all, Jesus praises this woman because it was she who made him aware of his prejudices. Jesus himself had to convert to the foreigners, to women, to what their society considerd dogs, that is, undesirable, unclean, evil.

The Canaanite woman resists and shuns all conventions which are far from representing a plentiful life for everybody. With her shameless behavior and persistence, she was being highly critical of the religious traditions and political institutions. Jesus humbled himself

72

regarding his personal biases and granted her request and Mark recorded that encounter for us to learn the lesson. Matthew even considered her a "woman of great faith."

To put it more simply:
This story of the dog Woman is a warning for us to be aware of our own prejudices.

Let us have an attentive ear in identifying current Syrophoenician women. We have to listen, for example to Rastas, the movement of the Caribbean islands, originated in Jamaica, where people protest against the ruling classes of society by means of reggae music or Bob Marley's songs, oriented toward social justice. We can see in our St. Croix streets people with long long disheveled braids and very unconventional dress, resisting a religion and a society that builds so many barriers between people.

The Syrophoenician woman is the message of overcoming prejudice that separates people. Jesus belongs to everybody, he loves foreigners, women, the sick, and people from other religions.

It was hard for Jesus to realize his own prejudices, to be aware that all human beings are equal before God, to experience the truth that God does not have favorites.

Who knows! perhaps the Syrophoenician woman in her powerful discussion, played a check mate to Jesus by quoting the story of her country woman, the widow, her son and the Prophet Elijah. That phoenician widow sacrificed her and her son by feeding Elijah with literally, her "last meal." (1 Kings 17.1-24).

May God grant us the disarming obstinacy and boldness of the Syrophoenician woman who defeated Jesus in a verbal combat!

Second Part
The Liturgical Year

18
NOT ALL THAT GLITTERS IS GOLD
Luke 21.25-36

"City of Goiania, Brazil, September, 1987: two garbage collectors find an abandoned metal pipe. They break it by hammering it and discover a stone with a white light. The magic stone transpires light, it is kind of bluelish and it makes everything the stone touches shine.

The two men break it into pieces, the fireflies made out of stone and share little pieces with their neighbors. The people who rub the stone on their skin will have their whole body shine at night. All the neighborhood is like a lamp. The poor people all of a sudden are rich in light, everybody celebrates.

The following day the two garbage collectors are vomiting. They ate mango and coconut seeds: without any doubt, that is the reason. But the whole neighborhood is vomiting too, all of them swell up, while an inside burning fire is burning their bodies. The light devours, mutilates and kills; and the light spreads out due to the air, the rain, the flies and the birds.

It was the biggest nuclear catastrophe in history after Chernobyl. Many people died, who knows how many; other people, the larger number became useless for ever. In this neighborhood on the outskirts of Goiania nobody knew what the word "radioactivity" meant, and nobody had ever heard talk about cesium 137.

The clinic which threw the pipe of cesium in the garbage continues operating normally, nobody was charged for this horrendous crime. Chernobyl is remembered everyday all over the world. About Goiania nobody says anything.

Some months after that, Cuba received the Goiania children who were affected by the radioactivity, and provided them free treatment. But this news also was not broadcast, as usual."[27]

Today we Christians are celebrating the beginning of the liturgical year. This is the first Sunday of Advent and the first Sunday of the Christian year.

Advent mainly means that Jesus is coming and with him, is coming a kingdom of sisterhood and brotherhood. In fact there are two advents, the one that took place 2000 years ago and the one that is going to take place some day.

Let's take a look at both:

I. The First Advent

This advent, or the coming one, points to the Christmas day. Unfortunately it seems that this Christian feast has been contaminated with radioactivity because it also shines with artificial and deceiving lights.

It started the day after Thanksgiving, or what is called "the black Friday" because it is the best day for selling. We are bored with the color of our walls, with our furniture, with our clothes, and in some cases even with our partners! People go shopping and shopping, all the sales and clearances just disappear. Some people stay overnight outside the stores in order to be the first in taking advantage of the special sales. During that day all the numbers of the account books of the businesses turn black, they recover from red numbers. In fact, Christmas started with the consumerism of that day. Christmas is similar to the panic shopping of "black Friday."

After that comes Santa Claus, the idol of buying. Children start learning from an early age that Christmas means Santa Claus. The only god for Santa Claus is his stomach. Santa Claus is the children's god. Santa Claus is the consumeristic religion. We don't realize that "not all that glitters is gold!"

Advent originally was a preparatory season for Christmas. First there were 7 weeks, later the church shortened it to 4. And the main purpose was to build the right environment for the celebration of Jesus's birth. It was supposed to be a time of Bible meditation, of prayer, of sharing with the family, of sharing with the neighborhood.

Now, let me go to:

II. The Second Advent

Every time we celebrate Communion we say: "every time you eat of this bread and drink from this cup, the Lord's death you announce until he comes again." That means that Jesus Christ is coming again! And it is precisely the theme of Advent, Jesus is coming again!

We don't know when, and we really don't need to know that date. What matters is that Jesus is coming again and from that day on we won't have to celebrate communion because we'll be sitting with him personally.

This season of 4 preparatory Sundays is then a time for us to be intentional in getting ready for Jesus Christ's Advent. We have to be ready at all times because nobody knows when he will return. And to be ready means to be fair, loving, caring, sharing. It is not for nothing that the table is also the constant reminder of Jesus Christ's Advent, where all his disciles will have a seat in the banquet at the end of the time.

To Put It Differently:

We are one month away from the 21^{rst} century. The 20th century was a cruel period of time. In 1997 alone, the USA and Europe spent 780 billion on the weapon industry, a trillion on the advertisement industry, 105 billion on the alcohol business, 50 billion on tobacco, 17 billion on food for pets[28], 13 billion on cosmetics, while more than 800 million people go hungry on our planet.

Who cared about the radioactivity of Goiania besides the song of

Rubén Blades and novel of Gioconda Belli? Lots of Brazilians were devoured by the brightness of that mortal substance. What happened with those fellows from Goiania seems to be similar with our current T.V., consumeristic society. Starting with the "black Friday," the day after Thanksgiving, everything and everywhere shines! The malls are to the top with lights. The presence of Santa Claus fills every place and every time, encouraging us to exchange presents, to buy lots of things for ourselves cause, "we deserve the best," etc. But in the midst of so much glitter we're losing the meaning of Christmas because "not all that glitters is gold!"

Well, Advent is a time for thinking and doing something about it. It was precisely during the advent season of 1511 in the city of Santo Domingo, that fray Antonio Montesino confronted his people with his powerful preaching. Don Diego Colón, the vice-governor and the cream of the crop was present. Montesinos raised his prophetic voice. "With what right and with what justice have you enslaved and treated these people so cruelly? With what authority have you declared such repulsive wars to these people, who were in their calm and pacific lands, where you have devoured with endless wars, killing and ravage unheard of before? How is it that you have them so oppressed and fatigued, without anything to eat, without taking care of their sickness, which is a result of the excessive work you demand of them, and the cause of their death? Better said, you kill them for the sake of getting gold every day."

Jesus Christ is coming again to be in solidarity with the garbage collectors, with peasants, with the suffering people. One African-American song got the point when it says with assurance: Children, we shall be free/ When the Lord shall appear/ Give ease to the sick, give sight to the blind,/ Enable the cripple to walk;/ He'll raise the dead from under the earth,/ And give them permission to talk.

19

ASSAULT UPON THE TEMPLE
Matthew 3.1-12

Today is the Second Sunday in Advent. This is a preparatory season for the celebration of Jesus Christ's second coming. Jesus Christ, who, as the Son of God was rich, made himself poor in order to enrich all humankind. One emphasis of the Advent season, then, is to thank God for his gracious love for all humanity.

This is precisely the message of John the Baptist, a message of God's gracious salvation for everybody. Let's take a look at how salvation, and its mediator the temple, has been interpreted in Jesus' time, in Danish West Indies' time and in our current time.

I. The Temple In Jesus' Time

The temple had not been used exclusively to worship God. The temple had also been used as a fortress, to support military missions. The temple had been used as banks, to keep and increase the treasury of the ruling class. The temple had been used as a court house, to apply justice to the people. And also the temple had been used as an archive to keep track of the debts of the entire Jewish society. Not surprisingly, when gangs assaulted the temple, first thing they did was to burn the debt archives of the people. Unfortunately for the poor people, the leaders of the temple usually had duplicates of the debt archives elsewhere.

Sometimes we get the idea that people loved the Temple of Jerusalem, but nothing was further from the truth. The Temple was a hated institution, especially by the poor people, the ones who were not able to pay all the taxes, and as a consequence, their debts were registered in the temple's archives.

Well, this morning we find John the Baptist assaulting the temple, not by burning the debt archives, but by promoting an alternative way of salvation, quite different from the one offered in the Temple of Jerusalem.

John the Baptist is preaching salvation outsider the gates of Jerusalem. Right in the Jordan River, he is going against the authorities of the Temple who claim to hold the franchise of God's salvation. John is not only ignoring the Temple priests and theologians, he is calling them "brood of vipers" (v.7). John is a revolutionary who rejects the luxurious way of dressing of the priests and high priests. Instead, he chooses to wear clothes made of camel's hair, with a leather belt around his waist. John the Baptist is a civil disobedient who, instead of feasting on luxurious dishes with the top ecclesiastical leaders, raises his protest by eating locusts and wild honey.

Still more, John assaults the Temple by baptizing people in the River, without taking into account the Temple's record of debts of the baptized people. John the Baptist is not only baptizing for free, he is disregarding the debts of the people. He is not only declaring the forgiveness of sins but, above all, is declaring the forgiveness of their Temple economic debts!

John's task is ground breaking, in preparation for Jesus' own assault on the Temple's debt archives. On that occasion, our Liberator Jesus Christ stated: "My Temple will be called a house of prayer. But you are making it a cave for thieves!." (Mt 21.13)

Now, let us consider:

II. The Temple in Danish West Indies' Time

When in the month of April –not January– the Portuguese stumbled with the coast of Brazil they confused a branch of the sea with a river and baptized it "Rio de Janeiro." Spaniards made the same mistake when approaching St. Croix Island by creating the "Salt River." Anyhow, pretty close to this "River" there is a hill called "Kierkegaard."[29] I like to think that it refers to Søren Kierkegaard, a Danish Lutheran pastor. By the mid 19th century, his ex-fiancé Regina Olsen married the West Indies governor and came to live on these Islands. Who knows, maybe she showed her feelings of love to her ex-fiancé by naming this hill after him! What is sure is that in his native city of Copenhagen there is not a single important street named after one of the greatest Danes. On the 23rd Sunday after Pentecost, Søren Kierkegaard is honored as a teacher and theologian. Nevertheless, the Christian calendar misses his prophetic character as a radical reformer of church and society!

The reason is that he was the John the Baptist of the Danes. He also broke his ties with the Temple, which only favored the wealthy and didn't care about the poor peasants.

In Denmark, confirmation mattered more than baptism. The confirmation certificate was like our social security number today. It was only through the Lutheran confirmation certificate that people reached their legal adulthood. Only by means of this document were people able to get married, to enter into contractual relationships, to enter a guild, to change one's place of residency, to travel about the country, to study at the university, to have access to the vast employment opportunities, or as Kiekegaard briefly comments, "the certificate the pastor issues, without which the boy or girl concerned cannot succeed at all."[30]

Pastors often owned the largest independent farms in the parish. They often held the sole library in the community. The job description of the activities of the local pastors was the following. Besides their church responsibilities, they were in charge of "collecting taxes; taking the census; helping to administer military levies; keeping the parish register of births, deaths, marriages and confirmations; supervising and inspecting the local schools; encouraging agricultural innovation;

83

supervising the poor relief system in the parish, a position in which the pastor could exercise great discretionary power, and, after 1841, serving as chairman of the local councils under legislation which extended limited self-government to rural districts."[31]

In this light, when Kierkegaard addresses the issue of the clergy, he has in mind the symbol that represents the authority of the crown and the well-educated people. The pastors legitimized the social order instead of reflecting on the suffering Christ. Like John the Baptist, Kierkegaard raised his voice by saying: "the pastor pronounces a blessing on the Christian society, this Christian state, where one cheats as in paganism, and by paying the pastor, thus, the biggest cheater cheatingly makes out that this is Christianity."[32]

Like in John the Baptist and Kierkegaard's generations, ours is also a "brood of vipers." Our generation also considers people to be sinful for not being able to pay their economic debt. It is a society where church, state and multinational corporations agree on oppressing the poor.

It was easy for J.P. Morgan, the leading banker of New York, to fight the economic panic of 1907, by using the church to strengthen the economy. Morgan just sent this message to the protestant pastors: "It is time for reaffirming faith. Beseech your congregations on Sunday to leave their money in the banks."[33]

Let me get it straight:

Advent is a preparatory season for Jesus Christ's coming! Jesus Christ emptied himself by giving his life for the liberation of all humanity. However, we human beings prefer to fill this Advent season with lots of noise, with the nonsense novels of Harry Potter, with the 15 months of celebration of the 100th anniversary of Walt Disney. And we don't want to face the crude reality. Every 24 hours 70,000 people died due to poverty. In Africa's Sub Sahara people live an average of 50 years whereas in Japan people's life expectancy is 80

84

years. In the Northern countries there is one physician per 400 inhabitants whereas in Africa's Sub Sahara there is only one physician per 13,000 people.

John the Baptist's conclusion says: "Even now the ax is lying at the root of the trees; every tree therefore that does not bear good fruit is cut down and thrown into the fire."

Our selfish society, blessed by false church leaders, encourages us to forget about what is going on in the world, but John the Baptist's message is to live fruitful lives by going out of the church, out to the river, to meet the people who can't afford to pay the bills, who are considered sinful because they can't buy or sell anything, the poor people that can't get a green card.

John the Baptist and Soren Kierkegaard are but a "voice in the desert." Let us join our voices with their voices, let us live fruitful lives, let us get ready for our Liberator's second coming!

20
BLIND BELIEF
Matthew 11.2-11

Once upon a time there was a French Man who went back home after a regular trip and first thing he found was his wife with her lover. His wife reacted spontaneously: "My love, I'm so glad your back." The husband angrily rebuked her: "how can you dare to call me 'my love' while you're cheating me under my very nose?' The wife, with tears in her eyes stated: 'Now finally, I realize you don't love me anymore, because you prefer to believe what you see and not to believe what you hear!'"[34]

This crude tale has the purpose of showing us how our society encourages "blind belief." "Blind belief" is one of the problems we find in the gospel and in general in our society: "should we believe what we hear or should we believe what we see?"

This is our 3rd Sunday in Advent. Our lectionary is leading our thoughts again, toward the meditation of the life of John the Baptist as a powerful forerunner of Jesus Christ's advent. However, this time John the Baptist seems to give room for "blind belief": "like the French man, should he believe what he hears or better should he believe what he sees?"

Albert Memmi, the Northen African professor of philosophy at the French Sorbone University is very enlightening in his analysis of "critical belief." Albert Memmi was an African scholar born in Tunisia, who consacrated his life to oppose "blind belief' by teaching us not to be satisfied with what we hear reality is, but with the reality we need to learn to see. One of the best books of this African fellow that helps us to denounce "pernicious believe" is his *Portrait of the Colonized People*.[35]

Now, what does Memmi have to say regarding our Gospel story? Let me focus on three examples of blind belief: The sexualization of sin; the profesionalization of Ministry and the manipulation of prestige:

I. Sexualization of Sin

Pernicious belief has told us that John the Baptist was imprisoned and eventually beheaded due to his disaproval of Herod Antipas' marriage with Herodias, his half brother's wife.

Thanks to the liberating thought of Albert Memmi we realize that John the Baptist was in jail and eventually would receive the death penalty due to very, very different reasons than the one of confronting the King for marrying his sister-in-law.

For instance, last Sunday we saw John gaining his surname "immerser" for baptizing and forgiving the sins of the people right out in the Jordan river. What John actually was doing was to ignore the Temple's oppressing debts which keep the poor people away from the Temple and away from heaven. John disregarded the Temple's monopoly of salvation.[36] Instead of that, he was telling the people that God was on their side and that their debts were forgiven. No wonder John the Baptist was put into jail and sentenced to death.

However, our sex-centered society still prefers to believe what it hears, that John was killed because he denounced the King's sexual misconduct. Unfortunately still our society reduces the ten commandments to the one which regulates our sexual life and completely forgets about the other nine commandments. "Pernicious belief" then is the sexualization of sin, but with Memmi we discover that what really is at stake is John the Baptist's forgiving economic debts as he stated in Luke 3. 10-11: "Whoever has two shirts must give one to the person who has none, and whoever has food must share it." Memmi convinces us that Freud was wrong, "sex is not

87

the essence of human beings." "Pernicious belief" tells us to explain this story in sexual terms; critical belief invites us to really see reality.

II. Professionalization of Ministry

The gospel passage for today has like seven verbs and nouns related with seeing and a couple of verbs regarding hearing. This is in fact like an invitation to pay more attention to seeing reality than to hearing about reality.

John the Baptist for a moment forgot about the need to see reality together with listening about reality, and showed his "blind belief": "Are you the one who is to come, or are we to wait for another?" John's "Blind belief" is requesting Jesus' curriculum vitae: does he belong to a "good family", does he owns a doctorate? Jesus has to fill up dozens of forms together with his psycological exam in order to be aproved by the examining committee! John the Baptist has fallen into the trap of "blind belief" by focusing more on hearing than on seeing; by focusing more on external conditions than on Jesus liberating deeds!

Memmi likewise tells us how in Tunisia the "French culture and white supremacist" physicians blame Africans even for ridiculous things like "not breathing properly", and psychiatrists explain African neurosis as a problem of their "North African souls."[37] What happened to John is what happens to us when we go to a doctor's office. The first thing that impacts us is the dozens of awards and titles hanging on the wall. We are under the spell of those luxuriously framed diplomas and we don't really see the inhumane attitudes and money making career of lots of physicians. "Blind belief" only hears what the titles say but never questions the cruel behaviors we really see.

88

III. Manipulation of Prestige

John the Baptist was in jail. Herod Antipas ordered his

imprisonment. Herod Antipas was in charge of the government of Galilee and Perea, East of Jordan river. Following the steps of his father King Herod the Great, Antipas built the city of Tiberias on the shores of the Sea of Galilee, in honor of the Roman emperor Tiberius.

Tiberias was built after the image of a Greek city in order to tell his people: "hey, you're second class citizens. Your architecture is not worthwhile, your culture, your dishes, everything you have is inferior to the Greek and Roman cultures."

Memmi also raises his voice protesting the way his African Tunisia has a wryneck, that is, that their head is stiff, looking toward France the whole time and denying African culture. Memmi is upset that his folks imitate even the French tics.

"Blind belief" tells us that what we hear from the media is what counts. However, "critical thinking" warns us that we need to learn to see reality by analysing the way the ruling class makes us believe that everything that comes from the empire is much better than local culture.

In Wrapping Up:

"Pernicious belief" consists of accepting the confession of love of the unfaithful French woman as the truth, and of denying the fact that she was in bed with her lover right there, under her husband's very nose!

"Blind belief" consists of the questionaire that John the Baptist sent to Jesus in order to find out about Jesus' academic credentials, completely forgetting about Jesus liberating deeds: "Go and tell John what you hear and see: the blind receive their sight, the lame walk, the lepers are cleansed, the deaf hear, the dead are raised, and the poor have good news brought to them." (Isaiah 35.5-6, 61.1-2)

89

"Pernicious belief" consists of Herod Antipas' attitude of praising everything from the Empire and disregarding everything from the local culture as Herod expressed in his building of the Greek-Roman city of Tiberias right there in Galilee. Little wonder, according to present records, Jesus never visited that imperialistic city.

"Blind belief" consists nowadays in believing as true what we hear or see on TV, and of denying as inexistent what we see in the streets and in real life. For instance, Johnny Weissmuller, the classic performer of Tarzan made his home in Acapulco, Mexico. After passing away somebody asked his wife if her husband really believed he was Tarzan. The widow shouted: "My husband didn't believe he was Tarzan. He *was* Tarzan indeed."

In the earlier sixties while visiting Disneyland, Billy Graham congratulated Walt Disney for building such a world of fantasy. Mickey's creator just replied: "Billy, this is the real world, fantasy is what is outside."[38]

The liberating good news of Jesus Christ is this: don't promote "pernicious belief." Don't believe just what you hear or watch on TV. Most importantly, rather than fantasies and more fantasies, we should believe what we see in real life. Our fantasy oriented society pays homage to the cream of the crop. Inversely, Jesus Christ honored John the Baptist, as the greatest of all human beings, in spite of his lack of taste in clothing and his diet of insects. And still more, Jesus tells us that: "the least in the kingdom of heaven is greater than John the Baptist."

"Blessed is anyone who takes no offense in me."

90

21
THE LAST WILL BE THE FIRST!
Luke 3.7-18; Mark10.31

Finally, after 36 days of being in the political limbo or in the political purgatory, 5 aging judges declared Bush as the new president of the USA. I sense that for the minority groups this was not what they expected. The minority groups which are used to playing secondary roles in society had focused their hopes on Gore, the vice-president. Perhaps, since we know first hand, what it means to be overshadowed by many clintons, we are especially sensitive to people who, after being in the background are now able to reach the front page.

This is the case in the gospel reading for this Sunday. We, minorities have the tendency to honor more John the Baptist than Jesus of Nazareth himself! Maybe without knowing, but in a correct way, we are applying Mark 10.31: "the last will be the first." In this advent season, a time for preparing our hearts for Jesus' Second Coming, let us meditate for a moment about John whose surename was "the Baptist."

It seems that we have learned very well, and very quickly, the lesson from Jesus Christ: "The last will be the first." Consciously or unconsciously we have favored John the Baptist, the precursor, the one who was not good enough even to untie Jesus' sandals." We have favored John the Baptist over the very same Jesus, isn't it a heresy? Not at all, it is to follow Jesus will: "the last will be the first."

This is not to say, "hey, now is my turn to rule and your turn to obey me." No, No. It is to say, in the Kingdom of God everybody is equally important. "The last will be the first" is not to encourage the oppressive vicious circle: "daddy abusing mommy, mommy mistreating children, children kicking the dog, and the dog biting daddy." "The last will be the first" means that all human beings are equally adorable and charming in the Kingdom of God.

Allow me to mention some examples of the way, we minorities have promoted John the Baptist to a more satisfactory role in society.

Some of the early Christian leaders like Origen, Ambrose and Leo the Great, esteemed John's role so highly that they said he was given "pre-natal grace" by God during the Visitation to Mary." (Lk 1.41)

Christianity and Caribbean traditional religions have in common the precious feast of John the Baptist. On June the 24th, Christianity, Santeria and Voodoo coincide in honoring him. Puerto Rico, in fact, has John the Baptist as its patron saint.

On June the 24th, many unmarried women ask for divination on this day, in order to find out whether they will marry somebody in the future. Brazilians portray John the Baptist as a falling in love handsome young fellow.

On this day, Christians and non Christians go to the beach to bathe in seawater. Under the patronage of St. John the Baptist everybody has a kind of "rebaptism." Whether we are conscious or not, at least the beaches of Puerto Rico are crowded that day.

In Jamaica, the Native Baptist recreated Christianity by taking into account the richness of African religious wisdom. For them too, John the Baptist is more important than Jesus Christ, since they reasoned that as John baptized Jesus, he must have had more authority. Native Baptists in Jamaica still sing: John a Baptist—Do my Lord/ Me pray for sin— Do my Lord/ Me pray for my soul—Do my Lord/ Remember your duty—Do my Lord/ Sinner dead he must—Do my Lord/ Me pray for keep me out of the fire—Do my Lord."

Now

92

Let us go back to Jesus' saying: "the last will be the first."

John the Baptist is known for being the forerunner, the precursor, the person in charge of the political and religious campaign of his cousin Jesus of Nazareth. John the Baptist has been portrayed as a humble person willing to step aside and act as a signpost to one even greater than himself. In other words, John the Baptist was born in order to serve others, in order to always play a secondary role, in order to always have a derivative value from somebody else. In order to live in the shadow, in the background. In fact, he had a sorry end. John was imprisoned and executed by Herod Antipas in about the year 28.

But, the liberating news is that there is another way of focusing on John the Baptist, and this different interpretation is especially done by minorities who know, in their own skin, what it means to be confined to play a secondary role in society.

John was not a soft person at all. He confronted his people by telling them that the way to prepare for Christmas, that is, the way to wait for Jesus is: "whoever has two shirts must give one to the person who has none, and whoever has food must share it."(10-11) Still more, John the Baptist addressed the most difficult people, the tax collectors and the soldiers, and told them right away that, to be ready for the first Christmas, they had to be fair: "do not overcharge, do not abuse the power you have, do not accuse falsely, do not seek bribes." (13-14) Instead of that, the Baptist told them to share.

John the Baptist had a mind of his own. He is considered the last of the prophets, but Jesus speaks of John as not only a prophet but "much more than a prophet." He also says that "no one born of a woman is greater than John; yet the least in God's kingdom is greater than he."(Mt 11.11, Lk. 7.28)

93

John the Baptist confronted the very Kingdom of Herod. He aroused people by his sermons. He drained the Temple's prestige and power by baptizing people in the Jordan and not in Jerusalem, this was a clear calculated alternative to the salvation system of the priests from the Temple. The people who followed him represented a form of sedition or even an uprising. John the Baptist preaching about the close coming of the Kingdom of the avenging God, was a real threat to the Kingdom of Herod.

"The last will be the first" is the egalitarian mark of the Kingdom of God. John the Baptist, and any of us, are invited to sit at the egalitarian table of Jesus Christ: No more secondary roles, no more subordination, no more having a derivative value, this is the liberating news of Jesus Christ!

94

22
THE MAGNIFICAT
Luke 1. 46-55

Luke was a theologian, a historian, and also a musician. During Jesus's birth alone the gospel of Luke included four songs: The Benedictus by Zechariah (1.68-79), The "Gloria in Excelsis Deo" by the Angels (2.14), The "Nunc Dimittis" by Simeon (2.29-32), and The Magnificat by Mary (1.46-55).

Let's take a look only at the fourth Christmas song called The Magnificat:

This is a hymn of social justice. Unfortunately many Christmas songs have been commercialized and many others don't promote the values of the Kingdom of God but only the nonsense of selfishness, so sweet and rosy stories and so on.

Mary had to face her small village. Nazareth was a tiny hamlet of a few hundred people. They gossiped about Mary's pregnancy. Celsus (end of 2nd century), a reknown philosopher, was of the opinion that Jesus' father was Panthera, a Roman soldier.

Mary had to face poverty. Jesus belonged to the artisan class which was located below the peasantry in the social pyramid.

Mary was a women who remained with her Son Jesus until his very scandalous death on the cross. Mary, the prophet and mother, could foresee the cross even from her child's birth.

Instead of a baby song, Mary sang:

"God has brought down the mighty kings from their thrones, and lifted up the lowly. He has filled the hungry with good things, and sent the rich away with empty hands..."

Martin Luther, in commenting Mary's "Magnificat" said that Mary belonged to a poor family and that she was in charge of taking care of the house and the cattle and that the high priest Caiphas' daughter never would have hired Mary not even as her lowest servant. Luther put "The Magnificat" hymn together with the social message of the Old Testament prophets of denouncing economic injustice. Luther said: "nobody but Mary could disapprove wealth and scare the wealthy in such a threatening way with God's curse of sending them with empty hands." In commenting the Magnificat, Luther quoted some German proverbs: "a prince is a rare bird in heaven" or "rich here, poor there." Luther called the stingy and covet people "worshipers of the stomach" because their god is their stomach. Luther praises Mary for promoting the well being for everybody and says: "A governor loses its cause if instead of working for the well being of his people, he just cares about having a good time only for himself."

In Mexico, Mary and the Magnificat contributed to abolish slavery, to distribute lands to the peasants, to stop paying tribute.

In Puerto Rico, Mary has been portrayed as an Afro-Caribbean lady since the 16th century. She was the protector of the run-away slaves. Mary was the milk mother of the three Kings. In the traditional picture of the three Kings, Baltazar is an Afro who had to be Muslim and not Christian. In the three Puerto Rican Kings, Melchor is Afro, and Christian, and always placed in the center as Mary's favorite.

In Jamaica first, and later all over the Caribbean Sea and beyond it, Mary's Magnificat took the form of reggae songs of protest, popularized by Bob Marley, Ras Akyem Ramsey and Ras Ishi in Barbados. Like the Magnificat Christmas song, Reggae music addresses social and political problems:

"This couldn't be my home
It must be somewhere else
Can't get no clothes to wear

Can't get no food to eat
Can't get a job to get bread
That's why I've got to go back home."

In St. Croix we have examples of brave and sensitive women like Mary of the Magnificat in people like her namesake, Queen Mary, the champion of social justice.

To put it most simply:
Our God is a God who sings.

Therefore, Christmas is also a season for singing. But singing is not an end in itself, it is a matter of singing in order to envision a better society.

John Newton, a slave trader and later Anglican pastor wrote many hymns like "Amazing Grace" but from quite another perspective. He used to fast, to pray and to compose hymns to praise God, for God to take care of the ships which transported "human flesh" so that they would arrive safely in order to make a good business deal!

Mary of the Magnificat resists while she sings for the creation of a more human world. Mary of the Magnificat, as well as Crucian Queen Mary or the "Captain" are two women who teach us how to sing a song of hope, of liberation of the end of injustice.

Haiti, a sister country of 7.5 million of inhabitants, has 65% of unemployment. Their general income is of 250 dollars per year, and this sister Island has the lowest literacy of the Western world.

Let's put away the honey, commercialized, nonsense Christmas songs. Let us join our voices in the liberating hymns of Jamaican Bob Marley, Puerto Rican Lucecita Benitez, Panamenean Rubén Blades, Mexican Amparo Ochoa, Cuban Silvio Rodríguez, Sonia Silvestre from Dominican Republic, ...

97

23

CAN ANYTHING GOOD COME FROM NAZARETH?

John 1.46

"What has he [Jesus] done about his future? Nothing. Does he have a permanent job? No. What are his prospects? None. To mention only this simple matter, how will he pass the time when he becomes old, the long winter evenings —with what will he fill them— he cannot even play cards... To join him —no, thanks, thank God I certainly have not gone crazy yet."[39]

This was the way a 19th century Lutheran pastor, Kierkegaard, used to critize the Danish Lutheran Church for continuing to believe Nathanael's pessimism: "Can anything good come from Nazareth?

Both of them, the Danish Lutheran Church and Nathanael had the right to raise their disbelief, because:

First:

I. Nazareth was an Illiterate Town.

The town of Nazareth, and the whole region of Galilee to whom Nazareth belonged, were an illiterate land. Galilean folks were not allowed to pray in the synagogues because of their mispronunciation and misreading. They neither spoke the language of the empire, namely, Latin, nor the language of the academia, that is, Greek. Galileans not even spoke standard Hebrew. They spoke a dialect of Aramaic.

Peter betrayed Jesus Christ three times, but Peter´s Galilean strong accent betrayed him three times, too. Galileans were blamed for corrupting the Jewish language, and for being illiterate and underdeveloped.

Secondly:

II. Nazareth was a Gentile Town.

The entire region of Galilee was a crossroad for many cultures like the Arab, Fenician, Syriac, Greek, etc. And of course, many of them ended up marrying the local people and making their living right there.

Nazareth then had the bad reputation of being a blend of blends, of corrupting the purity of the Jewish blood. They were considered almost pagan for all that exchange with people from other cultures.

Third:

III. Nazareth was a Poor Town.

According to one saying of that time we can see how poor they were. "The daughters of Israel are comely, but poverty makes them repulsive."

Nazareth was an obscure small village lost in the midst of the mountains. Galilee was a land of rich resources but they were drained for other people to enjoy them. What Galilee had was in fact many slaves ready to work or to sell themselves in order to survive.

Following human appearances, we arrive at the conclusion that Nathanael's pessimism is unforgivable: "Can anything good come from Nazareth?" Nathanael didn't have the right to raise that question because, according to John 21.2, he himself was born in Cana of Galilee.

Nathanael suffered of a low self esteem. He had learned from the empire to internalize a sense of incapacity, a sense of unworthiness, of lack of expectations. Take for instance this hymn: "The rich man in his castle,/ The poor man at his gate,/ God made them high and lowly,/ and ordered their state."[40] "Can anything good come from Nazareth?"

99

Likewise, the movies, TV, and magazines brainwash us with thousands of images which portray the false standards of beauty and at every minute raise the tricky question: "Can anything good come from Nazareth?"

Our story ends with the command: Come and see!

Can any thing good come from Nazareth? was the tricky question which led Jamaican Saint Michael Roman Catholic Seminary to teach a European curriculum up until 1956: Latin, Gregorian music, European History, England language and literature. It was not until June 23, 1957 when Joseph Bertrand, the first native Roman Catholic priest, celebrated mass in the US Virgin Islands. It was not until recently, when the Virgin Islands, after four centuries of Lutheranism had its first native Lutheran pastors: Paul E. West and Claude Petersen, but none of them served in the Land of the Seven Flags!

This week I went to the Dominican Republic and I was able to visit one sugar cane plantation, where all the workers were from Haiti, the poorest nation in the Western Hemisphere. Right now there are thousands of Haitians who experience the sugar cane tormentor in the neighboring country. They can only afford one meal per day, in the evening. During the day they drink sugar cane juice to keep on working for a miserable payment. But in the midst of such cruel conditions, Haitians preach: "We are poor, it is true, but we have pride. We are poor, it is true, but we are courageous. We are poor, it is true, but we are people nonetheless. We know that God created us in his image, and we the poor, who are abused, who are mistrusted, we are proud to be made in God's image. That pride will make us fight like the armies of God until the light of deliverance appears."[41]

Brothers and sisters, the Gospel of this morning is inviting us to come and see. Never ever forget that God instead of sending his son to be born in Rome, the heart of the empire, God sent him to the small colony of the Jews. Instead for his Son to be born in the Palace

100

of Herod, God chose a smelly barn; instead of choosing a princess from Jerusalem, God chose Mary, a poor Galilean peasant girl. Instead of prefering an earthly father with a brilliant career God opted for a Galilean carpenter. Instead of Jesus starting his ministry in Jerusalem, in Athens, or in Rome, he began his professional career in Cana, a small village of Galilee. And finally, on Easter morning, he closed his ministry with these words: "Go and tell my brothers to go to Galilee, there they will see me." (Mt 28.7,10)

Verse 46 says that Phillip didn't want to argue with Nathanael's question, that made no sense. Phillip only told Nathanael: "Come and see."

You Crucians, inhabitants of the "Big Island" just take a look at the words of your national seal: "United in Pride and Hope." Just come and see your own Virgin Islander's heroes: Claude A. Benjamin member of the Songwriters Guild Hall of Fame. Rothschild Francis "our Great Liberator," the St. Thomian champion of V.I. self determination, of home rule instead of Congress rule, of civil government versus USA Navy government. Valmy Thomas the great Major League baseball player. Barbara Christian the feminist Afro-American novelist. St. Thomian Edward Wilmot Blyden, Crucian Hubert Henry Harrison and St. Thomian J. Raymond Jones the promoters of Pan-Africanism. D. Hamilton Jackson, the apostle of freedom of the press, of unionized workers and the voice of the peasants. Olasee Davis, ecologist, journalist and preacher. Archie Thomas with his "Yellow Bird" or his "Archie Buck 'em up."

Come and see!

101

24
THE SACRED FAMILY
Mark 1:4-11

The big news corporations are selling us now the case of the Cuban little boy Elián González. Using a lifesaver, Elián swam from Cuba on last November together with his mother and step father. Unfortunately both of them passed away and the little boy found himself in Miami, as an orphan and without his immediate family. Fortunately Elián still has his biological father, his grandpa and grandma, and his extensive family in Cuba, anxious to have him back. Elián's father not only shared with his deceased ex-wife the custody of the child, but also the love and caring for their son. So, the INS and the National Council of Churches are right in wanting to send back the boy to his father. However, the Cuban-Americans are blocking the path. They are surrounding the boy with expensive toys and things and the message they are sending all over the world is: "in Cuba Elián may have his father and extensive family, but in USA Elián has lots of things." Now, let´s see if the US Federal Court decides if the best for Elián is to go back to his family or to have lots of things in the States.

The history of the West Indies tells us that in the past centuries the planters were enemies of the family ties of their workers by selling their siblings to other plantations and other islands. The world would do good in listening to what the Bible says about the meaning of the family.

We Christians are in the midst of the celebration of the sacred family of Joseph, Mary and the children including little boy Jesus.

And now, this Sunday we're attending the baptism of Jesus where he introduces to us his extended family of godparents, cousins, nephews, etc. And in case we doubt that the baptism is related with belonging to a family; Jesus also introduces to us his heavenly family of his Father and Mother.

I. His Heavenly Mama

She appears in the bodily shape of a dove. 2000 years ago the people that attended Jesus' baptism got the message. The dove is a very ancient symbol for the Goddess of love. Now, spirit has a feminine gender in the Old Testament and in the New Testament is recognized as the Spirit of Love. The friends that surrounded Jesus in the Jordan River didn't have problems in associating the Great Mother, the Goddess of Love with the Holy Divine Dove.[42] In fact the dove has been the only animal that has been accepted as holy and as a Goddess of fertility and love in the Near East. The dove (*peristera, columba*) was always holy to them and religiously protected. Great towers (columbaria) were built for them in order for them to have a place to nest.

The dove has been the only symbol for the Holy Spirit allowed in the church. You can see it painted in the cupolas, in the altars, in our banners, linens and clerical cloths. Mama Holy Spirit is right here!

II. His Heavenly Papa

He witnessed Jesus' baptism and raised his voice: "You are my Son, the beloved; with you I am well pleased."

103

God the Father can't miss his Son's baptism. His living voice had a seat in the Jordan River. For the Jews the most important of our senses was hearing.

Throughout the Old Testament we hear the voice: "Listen Israel" and this Sunday we hear God's voice directed to Jesus: "You are my Son, the beloved; with you I am well pleased." God the Father was in continuous conversation with his Son during all his earthly ministry even to the end on the Mountain of Calvary.

III. The Sacred Family

Then it is not just Joseph, Mary and their children. There is also his extended family of aunts, sisters and brothers-in-law, etc. And there is also the Divine family of Papa, Mama and Jesus Christ.

Jesus valued the extended family. While he was living in Capernaum (Mt 9.1) at Peter's home, at least four generations were living together. That contrasts with many of our homes where there is only one generation. In the past the grand or great-grand fathers were in charge of transmitting the image, the culture, the values, the high self-esteem to the new generations but today many of our elderly men are living in senior homes and they are taking with them to the grave very rich wisdom that they are not able to hand down to other generations.

We need to resist the individualistic society which isolates us. In the extensive family the defects of daddy can be fixed by picking up the good image or the example of an uncle, a godparent, or another member of the family. In the past the plantation owners used to break the links between father and son, the little boys and girls were given away, bequeted, or sold, to other plantations, and put to work at an age of 5 or 6. But, what they didn't take into account was that the new fathers would take those sons and daughters as theirs and would print their own image in the just arrived sons and daughters, and most importantly, the new fathers would teach the children about the high price and high self-esteem they possessed as resemblers of God's image.

104

Christian churches have their baptismal fonts at the entrance of their buildings in order to remind us that to be baptized is to get into the family of God. To be baptized means to live in community, to expand our extensive family. To build strong family ties. Some couples are childless, but in the church they find children like Naquisha. In some families the mother is mother and father, or the father is father and mother, but both of them within the church find company and solidarity. In the church we find children, papas, mamas, sisters, brothers because in the church nobody is alone, because, by being baptized all of us have entered a living and caring community. Because our same God doesn't want to live in isolation; Godself is a loving family. When we are sitting at the communion table, Jesus is the one that is inviting us, but the Father is also sitting there blessing the meal and the Spirit is sitting too, being sure that nobody misses the joining of the family feast, because:

To be baptized is to live in community:
Martin Luther used to say: "every time I wash my face I remember my baptism." He as a good European of that time, was not used to taking a complete bath. Europeans in those days in fact, only took two full baths in their entire life: after birth and after passing away! Bathing was considered a sinful act; because it led to pleasure. It was until the widespread of TV that showering became customary in Europe. But any way, he wanted to tell us that every time we take our shower we should remember our baptism. Because our baptism points to our identity. And our baptism tells us that our God is a living family that continually is inviting us to live in community.

We live in a gadget oriented society, every time getting more and more individualistic. We hear everywhere: get this, "think of yourself." Buy this for you "because you are worth it." Gratify yourself with that, remember, "you have only yourself." Our present selfish society is always pressuring us to be things-centered.

The gospel of this morning tells us quite the contrary. To be baptized is to be people or family-oriented.

Let us take advantage of our family traditions' wisdom. Remember how the Virgin Islands families are rooted in strong family ties. How the elders used to sing and chant history through story telling. How mothers breast-fed their children for long periods of time. How

105

members of the family used to carry children for two or three years. How we are people-oriented by been touchy, kissing, talkative, laughing, jammin people.

But, above all, being baptized means living in a loving community. As singles, as childless couples, as divorced, as re-married, as blended families, as living on our own, in any situation, we are not alone. We belong to a loving and caring family, we should continue to do something to keep our ties strong. And, above all, we must live lives committed to serve the lovely lonely folks.

That is precisely what many Cuban-Americans have forgotten, having lots of things is secondary, the family comes first. Maybe it would be a good idea to use the same internet page of Cuban-Americans to send a message to the White House, but in order to remind all of them that, as it is illustrated in the Trinitarian Papa, Mama and Child family, THE FAMILY COMES FIRST.

106

25

PORTRAITS OF JESUS CHRIST FOR OUR 1999 JOURNEY

Matthew 2.13-23

We don't know who is the king that lies behind the name Kingshill. What we know is that Columbus took possesion of St. Croix in the name of king Fernando and queen Isabel the Catholic. We also know that St. Croix´s main highway is named queen Mary. And we know that behind the names of Frederiksted are nine Danish kings and behind Christiansted are ten kings from the same country. It seems that Denmark´s repertory of names is not very creative: 19 kings and more to come share just two names. But "that is another enchilada." What is important to notice here is that human beings in general love to multiply kings and queens, the book of Guiness is full of examples.

The Gospel reading for this Epiphany Sunday instead of multiplying kings, equips us with powerful images of Jesus Christ, which may be of inspiration for our new year 1999. Allow me to comment on only three of these portraits: Jesus as a refugee, as a "dead man walkin" and as a have-not man.

I. Jesus Christ as a Refugee, 13-15

Our lectionary interrupts the narrative of the visitors from the East or what we know as the wisemen kings. However, Matthew devotes the whole second chapter to these people. The presence of these foreign men reminds us of the birth of Jesus as an international event.

Jesus Christ was killed as a political enemy of the Roman empire. In this passage, we find him being persecuted by the civil authorities at a very early age. And it was Egypt, Africa, or what we call today the "Third World" which granted Jesus his "green card."

All lands are important, are mainland, but US or what you call the mainland has to be particularly sensitive to Christ's story because the USA -with the exception of Native Americans- is a land of refugees: political refugees, economic refugees, religious refugees, ideological refugees, etc. St. Croix is also a mainland of refugees particularly now when one third of its population is Hispanic. In this lovely Island and everywhere on the planet we have to be sympathetic to the foreigners, because Jesus himself experienced the toughness of being a political and economic refugee in Africa.

II. Jesus Christ as Politically Sentenced 16-18

Tradition has told us that the visitors from the East were kings, some mention 3, others 9, others are more generous and count 12. Our text tells us about the confrontation between Jesus´ kingdom of life and Herod´s kingdom of death.

Albert Camus believed that Jesus always walked with his head bowed because He never forgot that due to his birth many children were condemned to the death penalty. However, we can ascertain that Jesus Christ is still dying today every time a child dies because of hunger, or every time people are visiting the culture of death of our modern Herods.

The Kingdom of God is a kingdom of justice and life. Jesus Christ told us not to flee from the world but to pray: "Your kingdom come, your will be done on earth as it is in heaven." Jesus Christ does not encourage us to be indifferent towards the earthly reigns. On the contrary, he encourages us to oppose the Herods who kill people.

Herod the Great was by no means an atheist or a secularized person. In fact, he always had the name of God on the tip of his tongue. He was a very religious person often surrounded by the chief priests, and Herod in exchange, rebuilt the famous temple of

108

Jerusalem. Nonetheless, his deeds were evil. Jesus preferred mercy and justice rather than bloody money and the killing of people.

It is not for nothing that Mary's song of praise expressed: "God has brought down mighty kings from their thrones, and lifted up the lowly. He has filled the hungry with good things, and sent the rich away with empty hands." (Lk 1.52-53)

III. Jesus Christ as a Homeless 19-23

The Three Wise men were in solidarity with Joseph, Mary and Jesus, the have-nots, the homeless.

As time went by and Herod died, this political refugee family returned form Africa to Israel and made their home precisely in the underdeveloped region of Galilee (Mt 4).

It was in Nazareth where Jesus was rejected when he preached on the text that says: "The Spirit of the Lord is upon me, because he has chosen me to bring the good news to the poor. He has sent me to proclaim liberty to the captives and recovery of sight to the blind, to set the oppressed free and announce that the time has come when the Lord will save his people." (Lk 4.18-19)

"Can anything good come from Nazareth?" Nathaniel asked. (Jn1.45) And Jesus answered YES, when he took the side of the people who were considered non-persons: the poor, the foreigners, the ones who talked with broken language, the ones who lived on the wrong side of the tracks, the people who were taken for granted, "the dregs of society," the have-nots.

In Summing up:

Throughout this new year of 1999 let us take with us these three images of Christ Jesus as a refugee, as a Political sentenced and as a homeless.

The current Key cay used to be called the Protestant Cay because at one time in our Island of St.Croix Protestants were not allowed to be buried and they had to have their own cemetery in the Protestant Cay. Presently Virgin Islanders run the risk of dividing society between the *bornya* (born here) and the not *bornya* of the other sister islands.

St. Croix and USA citizens —with the exception of Native Americans— know very well by experience what to be a refugee means. The US needs people who are sympathetic towards foreigners and refugees because your ancestors were refugees in America, as Jesus found refuge in Africa. Our countries do not need more hate against foreigners but cities of refuge.

We, as Christians have to resist the Herods who promote the death penalty. We have to oppose kings, governments, and social structures which, even though they seem to be God-fearing and very religious like Herod, they still are under the spell of death and killing. USA is the world's kingdom where the death penalty is applied the most. Herod's human sacrifices are still a common practice all over the world. Herod's fascination for death is alive in the war propaganda; in the weapons industry you can even get by internet, in the Holywood films, in the "American *War* of Life."

1999 represents another opportunity to face our personal and collective responsibility with the refugees, those sentenced to the death penalty, the have-nots of society.

110

26

EPIPHANY FEAST
Matthew 2.1-11

On Thanksgiving Day all the malls are closed in order to clear our conscience and go crazy shopping the following day. Half a day of December 24 and the entire next day the malls are closed in order to release our guilty conscience for all the presents we exchanged on Christmas Day. January the 1st, and the 6th, the shopping centers close so that our conscience may have a break for all the toys we bought for the Three Kings Day.

Epiphany feast celebrates the "Three wise kings" in the Western hemisphere, and also celebrates Jesus' baptism in the Eastern hemisphere. The Three "magi" were the first gentiles to worship the child Jesus as the "King of the Jews." They also were the first Christian missionaries who spread the good news of Jesus Christ beyond Bethlehem frontiers.

Epiphany feast has to do with the political persecution of King Herod not against the Divine child, but against the political Messiah. No wonder in Puerto Rico the "Three Kings," Melchor, Gaspar and Baltazar, are related with political issues, for example: Traditionally the Three magi represent three countries or continents, and 3 ethnic backgrounds or races. The difference with Puertorrican magi is that, it is not Baltazar but Melchor the one from Africa, and, Melchor is not Muslim, he is Christian, meaning that it is OK for an African person to be king, to be Christian and to be at the center and not longer at the margin. Another big difference of the Puertorrican magi is that the Three kings are not riding a camel but horses. Horses, here at St. Croix is a symbol of racing, like in Kentucky is the symbol of the Derby. But in Jesus' time horses were symbols of royalty, and the Puertorrican Three kings are telling us precisely that; the Epiphany feast has political implications. The Divine Christmas child doesn't bother anybody whereas the Christmas political Messiah disturbs the modern Herods of our times.

This morning allow me to focus our attention on the fact that Epiphany Day is another Christian feast that has been emptied from its political meaning and instead of that, has been brutally commercialized by our consumeristic society.

Santa Claus dressing like a clown, is not satisfied yet. People continue living on credit with the excuse that the gifts of the Three magi of gold, frankincense and myrrh means to buy, to buy and to buy. Therefore, just this Christmas season the toy industry produced 80% of the toy annual production.

TV, which in the USA is worshiped on an average of 7 hours per person, is in charge of transforming the Epiphany feast into an excuse to do panic shopping. Children and adolescents are extremely easy to fall into the spell of TV, particularly through comics. If you ask a child in October what he/she is expecting for the Three kings to bring him or her, the child won't know because all of them are waiting for the fashion which will be advertised until November and December, but once they get their new toy, after a little while they will abandon it. Anyhow, you better get precisely the new toy, otherwise you're out of the club. Pokemon, Dragon Ball, Ramma, Furby, Buvy Mammy, picachu, scooter, are the new heroes of children. The 40-year-old Barbie, is the ultimate. First you buy the toy like a down payment, later come the endless accesories you have to buy throughout the year.

The Three nice, so dressed up and smiling kings are the new mall´s managers. The hundreds of thousands of sueing cases for the physical and emotional injuries some toys cause is not a problem for

112

them. They are so almighty that every time they produce more aggressive toys that poison the children's minds, telling them to enjoy cruelty, to kill people, to be insensitive, to smash the neighbor, to be a winner in life.

The toy industry spends half of the cost of the toy in propaganda. The omnipresence of TV and computers are evidence that the consumeristic society has won the battle. Nevertheless, the good news of the Gospel invites us to resist a society whose god is gold, and whose priests are the merchants, a society that transforms everything into merchandise.

The book of Revelation 21.21 tells us that in Jesus Christ's kingdom, "the street of his city will be of pure gold." For all the Herods of our modern time and for all the promoters of the consumeristic society, gold is their god. For Christians and for honest non-Christians represented by the Three magi, says Revelation, gold is to be stepped on. The golden streets means that gold is no longer an idol for Jesus' followers.

Please let me mention some examples of how gold is to be stepped on:

In the Dominican Republic Christmas dinner is a meal that is shared with the less fortunate people. Dominicans teach us to be in solidarity with the hungry.

In Colombia the presents of January the 6th are the responsibility of the godparents. Godparents are right there to help in the expenses of their new family. Godparents are like guardian angels. A child that has godparents really has four parents.

In Chile the "Pasch Traveler" shows up with presents on Christmas night. On January the 6th Chileans celebrate the "Afro Pasch" in order to honor the African king who visited Jesus.

113

In Costa Rica Christmas begins on December the 1st and finishes on Candlemass feast of February the 2nd. This season is especially meaningful for being a time to share food everywhere.

In Puerto Rico the three kings stay alive the whole year, filling the homes and places with joy, with lots of music, with art, with beauty, with hope for a better world.

In Mexico, on January 6, people get together to eat the Three Kings bread with hot chocolate. Inside the round bread, there are 2 or 3 hidden baby Jesus dolls. The people who get the very little plastic doll, will prepare supper for February 2, during Candlemass Feast. The Three King's feast is a synonym of sharing the table.

In St. Croix a lively parade takes place on January 5 and 6. You have the particularity that instead of asking for presents you fill the Three Kings with presents right there at the Little Village. You also share guavaberry bread, the "real McCoy." (the authentic)

Let me put it this way:
Fathers and mothers, grandpas and grand mamas, let us ask God for wisdom to face the crude and cruel society. Reality is not like TV portrays it, not at all.

The Messiah of Händel has a sentence against pagans: "pagans are trembling" but the three magi are an example of how gentiles, pagans, foreigners are more generous, more pious, more tender and lovely than many that call themselves Christians. When the Messiah of Händel was sung for the first time in London in 1742, immediately after that singing the British troops departed to conquer India.[43] The message of Christmas and Epiphany is quite the opposite. It is not a message of conquering the pagans, it is a message of seeing and listening to how God accepts pagans, gentiles, foreigners like the Three magi, for being generous and true worshipers of the King Jesus Christ.

114

The Three magi as they are pictured on TV are values destroyers whose god is gold, buying, spending, killing. These Three TV magi pile up mountains of toys in a world of hunger. The Three TV magi don't avoid and don't stay away from Herod; on the contrary, they work for Herod in destroying children in many ways.

The Three magi of the gospel are an invitation to be generous, sharing, to be in solidarity with the unfortunate like the homeless Joseph, Mary and Jesus. The Three magi of the gospel don't listen to the lying voice of Herod but to the voice of God. It is unbelievable that in the midst of misery Imelda Marcos, the first lady of the Philippines ex-president Ferdinand Marcos, became famous all over the world for her collection of 3,000 pairs of shoes! Although she clarified: "I did not have three thousand pairs of shoes, I had one thousand and sixty."

Brothers and sisters let us stay away from the modern Herods, let us imitate the Three magi the whole year. All of us have gifts, skills, talents. Don't get tired to offer them to Jesus Christ, our Liberator.

115

27

TOUCHING, LIFTING, LAYING HANDS AND BLESSING
Mark 10.13-16

What I like the most of "Frederik Lutheran Church" of St. Thomas is not the fact that it is the second oldest Lutheran church in the whole continent, dated from 1666. I don't like the most neither its marble altar or its very high pulpit, nor its Danish architecture, nor its Christus Victor crucified on the wall. What I like the most are a stained glass window and a small sculpture of Jesus that are close to the altar. Those two art pieces contain the four key verbs: touching, lifting, laying hands and blessing of the children. In our case, those 4 strong verbs are related with Glenroy Cameran, Jaheem Cuencas, Abijah Isaac, and Charjanne Phipps.

A few years ago a letter dated June 18, 1c.e. was found on the west bank of the Nile about 120 miles south of Cairo. Hilarion, a menial worker wrote to his wife Alis:

"Hilarion to his sister Alis many greetings, likewise to my lady Berous [his mother in law?] and to Apollonarion [their first and male child]. Know that we are even yet in Alexandria. Do not worry if they all come back [except me] and I remain in Alexandria. I urge and entreat you, be concerned about the child [Apollonarion] and if I should receive my wages soon, I will send them up to you. If by chance you bear a son, if it is a boy, let it be, if it is a girl, cast it out [to die]. You have said to Aphrodisias, 'Do not forget me.' How can I forget you? Therefore I urge you not to worry." 29[Year] of Caesar [Augustus], Payni [month]23 [day] (June 18, 1 b.c.e.)[44]

What we get from this letter is that infants in general and little girls in particular, didn't count at all in Jesus' Mediterranean culture.

I. The Kingdom of Rome:

Every time a baby was born, he or she was presented to the father in order for him to decide whether to pardon him or her and let him or her live, or just to throw the new born baby to the streets. Unwanted babies were condemned to their own luck. Now, if the father forgave his little girl or little boy, then the father had to express it with his body language, through four key verbs: To touch, to lift the baby up, to lay his hands on, and to bless the baby. Touching, lifting, laying hands and blessing meant acceptance, forgiveness, to welcome the new born baby to life.

When Jesus fed the multitudes none of the gospel writers reported the number of children that were fed, because children didn't count. This morning we find some people bringing very probably street children, abandoned children to Jesus for him to accept them as human beings, but, it is not surprising to realize that the very disciples rejected the children.

The Romans didn't give names to their daughters but numbers. In the case of their sons, they started putting numbers after the third son. Every time a Roman child was born the baby was put at the father's feet. If the father touched, lifted, lay his hands and blessed the child, the baby would survive. If the father didn't lift (*suscipere*) the newborn baby, he or she was put out in the streets, this was the case especially of girls, the handicapped, and sick children. Many found death, some would be raised as slaves, as gladiators, and as prostitutes. Other thrown out children were mutilated in order to profit with them as beggars. Other cast out children were used as pets and also in the parties as comedians.

In Europe children who were not desired were abandoned either in shelters or simply at the front door of the churches, 94 % of them

117

usually died because of the cold temperatures of that continent. In the case of accepted children, they had to be baptized after 8 days of being born, but their mothers had to wait at home purifying themselves for 40 days. The godmother was in charge of taking the godchild to the church for receiving the baptism through touching, lifting, laying hands and blessing the child. When the baptism was over, again, the godmother took the godchild back to the mother who was waiting at the entrance of her home. The godmother delivered her child with the words: "you gave me a Muslim child, I returned to you a Christian child" meaning, you gave me an un-baptized child, I return you a baptized child. Then and only then, it was safe for everybody to kiss the already purified child.

In English and in Spanish we share the same word for child, infant. This word comes from Latin *infans* which means "the voiceless." Infants are children from birth to the beginning of their teens or adolescence. Infant is also applied to infantry soldiers, meaning that, either soldiers or children, are not allowed to talk, to speak is forbidden. They are voiceless even at this moment of the Yemen tragedy.

In the time of slavery, people were baptized before they were imprisoned in the ships. In that way, if somebody got sick, specially the little children, they were thrown into the sea but, through the Christian baptism, their eternal destiny was assured!

The time of slavery, the masters —always a man— had intercourse with our women ancestors, but the planters were very scrupulous, first our mothers had to be baptized because the Bible says: "Don´t join with the unbelievers." (2 Cor 6.14)

II. The Kingdom of God

The Kingdom of God as is presented by Jesus Christ is so shocking for the kingdom of Rome and even for the same disciples: What Jesus is really telling us is that the Kingdom of God is a Kingdom of nobodies. That what society doesn't count goes first in the Kingdom of God. What society throws away to the garbage, those human beings are more than welcome in the Kingdom of God.

United States of America is not really a name, it is a description, and a description of the whole continent. This is almost the case of the "country" of South Africa. On the other hand, we have learned to divide the American Continent in three sections: North, Central and South America. But what about the fourth region: the Caribbean? Those 24 countries, with their own food, music, dances, ways of celebrating, of walking, of dreaming, of fighting. 24 countries whose languages go from their own languages to the recreation of English, Spanish, French, Dutch, Danish, etc. In a map it is much easier to enjoy the 84 square mile silhoutte in the shape of a boot of St. Croix, the silhouette in the shape of a little pig on the brass (lechoncito asado) of Puerto Rico... than the silhouette of many countries. But still, people eliminate the fourth section because the Kingdom of Rome has told us that we don't count. However, in the Kingdom of God there is no such thing as geographical and biological inferiority.

Let me piggyback to our main point:

I am number 6 out of 7 children. My father, like Hilarion, wanted a baby boy. God and my mother gave him one, two, three, four boys. He got tired of boys since the third, therefore, he ordered to have the fourth dressed as a girl for two years until finally my sister showed up. Then came I, no big deal! I wasn't touched, lifted up, hands were not laid on me, but my father made up for it by blessing me with his name, Eliseo.

119

It is not for nothing that Jesus' four key verbs of touching, lifting, laying on of hands and blessing have been the center of baptismal ceremonies for centuries. Today we thank God because everybody who has been baptized is able to renew their baptism. Today everybody can experience again on his or her body the four key actions of Jesus: touching, lifting, laying on and blessing. And today four new baptized brothers and sisters will have the experience of being accepted, of being chosen to live, through these four action verbs of Jesus: touching, lifting, laying hands and blessing.

Welcome to an abundant life Glenroy Cameran, Jaheem Cuencas, Abijah Isaac, and Charjanne Phipps and Elijah Lincoln Vigas. Please tell them that they have been accepted by Jesus Christ. Please tell them that their rich Crucian history, culture, music, has been accepted by Jesus Christ. Please tell them that instead of a number they got a name like the Afro American song states:

Written down my name
Hush, somebody's calling my name
I've got a new name in Glory
and it's mine, all mine.

120

28
THE PURIFYING FIRE
Luke 2.22-24

The Feast of Candlemass started in Jerusalem from about 350 c.e., in Constantinople around 542 c.e., and in Rome by the year 700 c.e. As time went by Candlemass was associated with the blessing of candles, which the following day, on the Feast of Saint Blasius, were used to bless throats.

In Puerto Rico, on Candlemass Day people burn their dry Christmas trees, in order to bring light to this world through a joyful camp-fire! This is so, in order to honor Jesus Christ as the "light to lighten the Gentiles" from the canticle *Nunc Dimittis* (Luke 2.25-32).

In Mexico on January 6 , people gather to drink freshly whipped hot chocolate and eat the Three Kings bread. This consists of an oval-shaped roll. The top is nicely decorated with candied fruit, and inside there is a porcelain "chilpayatito" (baby) Jesus, placed at random. The person whose slice has the doll hidden inside, has to dress the "chilpayatito" on Candlemass Day in order to remove Jesus from the Nativity scene, and present him in the temple. Besides that, he or she has to invite the neighborhood to eat "tamales and atole" (both made out of corn, and both pre-Columbian).

Why don´t we revisit Candlemass in the Bible, in the Reformation and in Present time?

In the Bible

February the 2nd reminds us of the Feast of the presentation of Jesus to the temple and to the purification of Mary as well.

Unfortunately our lectionaries usually avoid dealing with this Marian Feast of her journey to Jerusalem for her purification.

Candlemass is the feast, if we can call it feast, because that points to the uncleanliness of women giving birth. Moses' law said that after the birth of a baby boy the mother was ceremonially unclean for 7 days, and needed 33 more days of isolation for her purification. In the case of a female child, the period was twice as long (Lev 12.1-5). This is the origin of the quarantine, from the Candlemass feast of cleanliness. After 40 or 80 days of the birth, poor women were supposed to offer a pigeon or 2 turtle doves (Lev 12.6-8) because they couldn't afford to buy a lamb.

As time went by, the church started taking the church doves and sandwiches in order to remember the pilgrimage to Jerusalem. Besides that, Christians took the most artistic and beautiful candles in order to be blessed at the church, and to place them in an important space of their homes during the whole year. They used to light them only during strong storms. From here takes the name this feast of Candlemass. For the Anglo-Saxon countries Candlemass day means a day that will allow them to predict the rest of winter season. If Candlemass is dry, the cold time will continue; if it rains during February the 2nd it means that a beautiful spring season is coming soon. We can add more lively meanings to this Marian Feast, but nevertheless, we have to address the seamy side of this celebration. Only Mary, and not Joseph, as an impure being, makes us realize the unfairness of women's condition. Matthew doesn't count women in his census, Moses counts women together with things and animals in the 10 commandments, etc. Jesus rebuked a woman who continued to consider that the role of women is solely of producing children: "Rather how happy are those who hear the word of God and obey it! " (Lk 11.27-28)

122

In the Reformation

Things didn't change substantially. To quote only one reformer,

Martin Luther, he was very appreciative of his wife Cathy and of the virgin Mary, but let's see his opinion on women expressed in his *Table Talk*.

In 1531 he stated: "Men have broad shoulders and narrow hips, and accordingly they possess intelligence. Women have narrow shoulders and broad hips. Women ought to stay at home, the way they were created indicates this, for they have broad hips and a wide fundament to sit upon, keep house and bear and raise children." By 1532 he insisted in his speech by expressing: "No good ever came out of female domination. God created Adam master and lord of all living creatures, but Eve spoiled it all." In 1533 he wrote: "Girls begin to talk and to stand on their feet sooner than boys because weeds always grow up more quickly than good crops." In 1538 he still persisted in his idea of women as impure persons: "Eloquence in women shouldn't be praised: it is more fitting for them to lisp and stammer. This is more becoming to them."

Martin Luther himself used to celebrate five Marian feasts, later he only kept three, including the Candlemass. But he never purified himself of his sin of considering men superior to women. The great reformer, like us men of this closing century, need the purifying fire of the equality of sexes.

In Recent Times

We men do have many motifs to ask for purification.

Due to the influence of European Christianity, the Candlemass Feast has been above all an occasion for the mistreating of women. One was allowed to kiss children exclusively after their baptism. Mothers were supposed to stay isolated at home for 40 days. Wealthy women didn't have problems with that, they just took off those days. Poor women had to go out almost immediately to make their living but they had to cover their head with a roof-tile in order to warn the others about their impurity. The Candlemass is still for many cultures a constant reminder of the uncleanliness of women's

123

blood, as if this precious women's blood were not of the same type of Jesus Christ's blood. The word *placenta* comes from Latin, which means dirtiness.

The European conquerors first had to baptize our colored women in order to purify them, and after that they raped them with a clear conscience. 85 % of the executions of the not so holy inquisition were of women. Married people use to be buried in dark coffins, the white ones were only for single persons. When a woman died, the bell rang 18 times, whereas when a man died, the bell rang 24 times. If a woman had remarried she didn't deserve neither prayers nor bell ringing in her burial. But there was no problem with a man who had remarried. Women had to cover not only their heads but also their hands in order to receive the communion bread, so that the priest was not tempted in touching the woman's flesh.

In the early Christian church mother's milk was a favorite symbol of the Eucharistic table: In a similar way in which we "ate" our mothers through their milk, Jesus Christ is nourishing us out of his body. Christ is nourishing us with lettuce, in Spanish "lechuga", that is, milky. Christ is nourishing the entire galaxy as its name says: "The milky way." Nonetheless, we men ought to purify our vision and thoughts. We extended the impurity period to the whole time of feeding the child. We prohibited women from taking communion when they were breast feeding. Again, women with economic means just needed to hire a "tetera" namely, a milkwoman, or a wetnurse, to feed their children, creating in this way the milk sisters and brothers. But the poor women had to wait years for the sacrament.

124

To bring the matter closer:

Moravian faith is an excellent antidote against Christian machism. Zinzendorf, the moravian founder, came to the Virgin Islands in 1739 to overview the mission. Now, together with the gospel of Jesus Christ, the Moravians brought the message of the "motherly ministry of the Holy Spirit." Zinzendorf was so sensitive to our loving Divine Mother, the giver of life, that he used to say: "It was improper that the motherly ministry of the Holy Spirit should have been disclosed to the sisters not by a sister but by me." Moravians even declare as a basic doctrine of their creed, the one of our loving Divine Mother. In places like Ethiopia they still zelously keep icons of the Holy Spirit as a "She."

Let us close this millennium and open the third one celebrating the everyday purifying fire of our attitudes. All over the world the Christian church is a church mainly of women but run by men. Thank God because Kingshill and Christus Victor Lutheran Churches have in many of your women great leaders. Thank God for the full time pastors you have had like William Montgomery, Earl Walker, David Rinas, Joseph Donnella, Robert Martensen, Stephen Alsleben, and Daniel Swanson. Now, who knows, maybe the time is coming for both congregations to get your first woman full pastor. Don't worry, sooner or later you're going to have it. In the meantime, let us continue purifying ourselves with the candles of Candlemass Feast.

29

MY LORD'S A-WRITTIN' ALL THE TIME!
John 20. 30-31

A protest Afro-American hymn says:
Come down, come down, my Lord, come down!
My Lord's a-writtin' all the time.
An' take me up to wear the crown!
My Lord's a-writtin' all the time!

This is exactly the case of the gospel of this morning. In the conclusion of his gospel John states: "There are many other things that Jesus did. If they were all written down one by one, I suppose that the whole world could not hold the books that would be written." And in today's gospel John repeats: "In his disciples' presence Jesus performed many other miracles which are not written down in this book. But these have been written in order that you may believe that Jesus is the Messiah, the Son of God, and that through your faith in him you may have life."

I know, I know, you may be asking by now: "why did the pastor read only part of the gospel lesson for this Sunday? Well, let me tell you, because I'm just following John's example of being selective!

John already warned us: "If I would write down all things Jesus performed, the whole world could not hold the books that would be written." Therefore, if I would write down my reflections about the four Bible passages we just read, two from the Old Testament and two from the New Testament, people would change 970 MW radio station. Then, I'm just following John's example of being selective! Like our lectionary which is also selective. Like the media which is also selective.

On the other hand, the African-American song says: "My Lord's a-writtin' all the time!" means, that God is also writing our history, that God remembers our history, that God tells our history!

We can raise at least two questions from these two verses of John 20.30-31. What are you writing, and Why are you writing? First:

I. What are you writing?

John had a lot of things to report about Jesus' ministry but what John did was to choose but a few of Jesus' deeds. In other words, John selected his own version of Jesus' history! It is not for nothing that the gospels of Matthew, Mark, and Luke are called the synoptic gospels, that is, the gospels that take a look at Jesus' ministry from the same angle. Whereas John's writing is done from a different point of view! To be sure, the 4 gospel writers are telling Jesus Christ's history from their own point of view, but John is the most conscious of being the most selective of them all, simply because he wrote after the other three.

Gustavo Gutiérrez, a Peruvian priest, said that history has been written by a wealthy, old, white, male hand. In short, history has been written by a winner's hand! However, John is reluctant to give up in terms of the writing of history. He himself chooses what fits his vital needs.

Today Dr. Ruth Beagles starts teaching our confirmation class a series of lessons related with Virgin Islands' Lutheranism. Now, there are so many things we can say about this theme, but the confirmation class will hear the selective teaching of Dr. Ruth Beagles. The children will hear a version of history written by a committed, Christian, Crucian, female hand. Dr. Beagles is writing a particular version of history, because all histories are particular, but unfortunately many

127

times the dominant version of history has been imposed on us, emptying us of our own wonderful history!

The other day Leopoldo Zea, a Mexican philosopher was in Paris, talking to Andre Malraux, a French novelist, who also visited a Maya and Aztec art exhibition. Malraux said to Leopoldo: "You must be very proud of your great Mayan and Aztec cultures, the same way we Europeans are proud of the Greek and Latin cultures." Leopoldo rushed to answer: "Excuse me, I think that we have more than you." Malraux got confused and asked: "What do you mean, you have more than us?" Leopoldo told him right away: "Are the Mayan and Aztec art yours?" The French said no. Leopoldo replied: "Well, we have the Mayan and Aztec cultures but we also have the Latin and Greek cultures, we have more than you." "You're right", the French novelist had to agree.[45]

Virgin Islanders have their own culture enriched by the African wisdom, by the Native ancestors, by the Seven European cultures. You must be very proud of your history! You have much more culture than the cultures which deny what is different from theirs.

You Virgin Islanders have your own music but you also have Mozart and Beethoven! You Virgin Islanders have your own cuisine but you also have Italian, French or Spaniard cuisine! You Virgin Islanders have your own history, but you also read universal history! Your culture is bigger and richer than the dominant culture which imposes its particular version to the detriment of others.

Now, let us go to our second point:

128

II. Why are you writing?

My Lord's a-writtin' all the time. An' take me up to 'wear the crown! Says the song, and the gospel says that John wrote down Jesus' deeds, not just because he wanted to sign his John Henry! Not because John pursued the Nobel prize in literature. They wrote in order for us to believe in Jesus Christ and through that to reach the fullness of life: "An' take me up to wear the crown!"

Why are we writing, reading or telling history? In order to reach life! An' take me up to wear the crown!

Every time our school textbooks omit the heroes and geography of Virgin Island history, something within us is dying. Every time our churches omit the African-American music, something within us is dying. Every time the University of the Virgin Islands omits the Caribbean studies, something within us is dying. While writing John had the purpose of promoting life! An' take me up to 'wear the crown!

John left out of his account many things related with the Greek and Roman cultures simply because those dominant cultures didn't need to be affirmed. John instead promoted life, through his selected historical facts related with his own culture. In our case we may leave out some things but we can never ever leave out our Afro-Crucian, our Puerto Rican-Crucian, our Santo Domingo-Crucian cultures because they are our life!: "An' take me up to 'wear the crown!"

I just love the way Afro-American and Pentecostal churches select history. While preaching you can tell what things the preacher can leave out because of the silence of the congregation. But, on the other hand, you punctuate by applause, cheers and other signs of support what makes sense: "Well," "I'm telling you," "Uuummm Hummm" "Hit Home," "Tell It," Right On, Preacher," "Sounds Good." "Preach Sister"... When you hear those voices you can tell that what you're saying is related to life! "An' take me up to 'wear the crown!"

129

Let me put it this way:

Keep in mind Barbara Christian, the V.I. feminist Black Woman Novelist. Harold Willocks, our Crucian Lutheran historian. Anna Marie Vessup, the activist who in 1935, gained women's right to vote in the Virgin Islands.

Remember European misleadings in associating the red-dye painting of faces and bodies of the West Indies Calina culture with the Devil. What Europeans didn´t realize was the fact that red-dye made out of crushed annatto seeds, was an excellent insect repellent and a fabulous anti-sun burn lotion!

Let us write our history with a local hand, with a female and a male hand, with a young and an old hand. Let us write and tell our history with a schooled hand and an unschooled mouth. Let us write, let us preach, let us tell our history by being very selective like John and like God:

"Come down, come down, my Lord, come down!

My Lord's a-writtin' all the time.

An' take me up to 'wear the crown!

My Lord's a-writtin' all the time!

130

30
WE ARE STAR POWDER!
Genesis. 3.19

When my mother gave birth to me, her first words were for my oldest brother: "hey, take the umbilical cord, go to the backyard and bury it."

That ritual, which is part of my culture, has the purpose of reminding us that one day all of us have to go back to the earth's womb. That some day all of us will be wrapped up again within the earth's womb! In the Hebrew language Adam, the name of the first man, comes from *adamá* meaning earth, dust, that is, we are the same earth. In Latin *humus* means fertile soil.

Now, the other day a Spaniard woman passed away. Before she died, she gave instructions that she wanted to be cremated and her ashes to be spread out in the mall. According to that Spaniard woman, the shopping center was the best place for her ashes because "she spent the most beautiful days of her life in the mall." Gen 3.19 meant for her: "remember you're merchandise, and to merchandise you'll return."

Last Wednesday some of you got the sign of the cross marked with ashes on your forehead, and you heard the sentence: "You're dust, and to dust you'll return."

Allow me to meditate a little bit on Ash Wednesday, as the beginning of Lent season, which starts precisely with the saying: "You're dust and to dust you'll return." In doing so, I propose to you two points: First, Dust as a sign of penitence, and second, Dust as a sign of brightness.

The first part says:

I. Dust, as a Sign of Penitence

In 1099 the pope Urban II, gave the name of Ash Wednesday to the first day of this preparatory season for Easter.

Ashes is a symbol of sadness and repentance that was used in the Old Testament and in the primitive church. Originally it was only the clergy, later only the public penitents, and finally, the ceremony where people spread ashes on their head and clothes was extended to everybody.

Dust, as a sign of penitence invites people to meditate about life, about repentance of sins, and especially about our lightness and short life.

We have been taught that, because of our sinful fall, God's curse consists of limiting our life and sending us back to the ugly dust! But that is not exactly what the Bible tells us.

Therefore, let me go to my second point:

II. Dust, as a Sign of Brightness!

The book of Genesis 3.19 says: "remember you're dust and to dust you'll return." That's correct. But, before saying that, the same book says in 1.31: "God looked at everything he had made, and he was very pleased." This means that the Earth is a fine art which pleased God a lot. This means that going back to dust is going back to God's beautiful creation! Dust is not something dirty or something low and despicable. Quite the opposite, *dust* in the book of Genesis means something good.

132

How many of you have observed the marvelous range of colors a sunset produces? And the most important, how many of us know that precisely that magnificent range of colors is the result of the contact between the sun rays and of all kinds of dust from the Earth![46] Some blurry days in Puerto Rico we say are due to the "Sahara powder." "Remember you're dust" of the dust of Ash Wednesday means then, remember you're beautiful.

It was until the last part of the 20th century that we finally got the point. Astrophysics, the science that studies the universe, allowed us for the first time to be able to tell the story of our planet Earth! The Earth used to be a sun, and suns are the same as stars. That sun once exploded and a very tiny piece of that explosion got cold and formed our planet Earth. That is why we can say, we are "children of one sun" or if you prefer: "we are star powder", "we are cosmic powder."

In the year of 1,600 the priest Giordano Bruno was burned alive in Rome by the "not so" Holy Inquisition. His sin was to declare that stars are suns; that matter is the mother of all living beings and that God is the "world-soul." Now we know he was right, and the Holy Inquisition, as often, was wrong!

In the delicious novel *Like Water for Chocolate*, the impossible love of Tita and Pedro finally found its way by means of a huge fire. Since human bodies contain the elements to produce phosphorus, their fiery bodies began to throw off glowing sparks reaching their divine origin.

Dust in the book of Genesis means that our Earth is a living being, is not a passive deposit of resources, something like: "help yourself." William Bowling understood very well the meaning of dust when he said: "Christ shed his blood also for cows and horses as for human beings."

To bring the matter closer:

To the question: what was God doing before He created the World? St. Augustine answered: "God was preparing hell for everyone who raised these kind of questions." St. Augustine's God of course, is not the loving and caring God of the Bible.

It is not up to us to know about what God was doing before He created the World! But one thing is for sure: what he created and still continues creating is the ultimate! God was so pleased with his

133

creation! We, human beings, were created out of clay, because dust is beautiful, dust is brightness!

A few years ago, a Bolivian Methodist pastor observed that one of his members poured out some drops from his cup into the soil every time he had communion. The pastor thought: "well, the easiest thing for me to do is either to ignore it or to prohibit him to continue pouring out the wine, but I'm going to have a guilty conscience." Once the pastor learned that his member's culture considered earth a living being in need of Christ's blood too, the following communion service the pastor had something in mind: "Brothers and sisters, at this time you may pour some drops of Jesus' blood on the soil, in order to fertilize it."[47]

Sisters and brothers, in this Lenten season let us meditate about this gorgeous thought: "Remember you're dust, and to dust you'll return." "Remember you're beautiful and to something beautiful you'll return."

Ash Wednesday and the Lenten season in general is also an invitation for all of us to remember about the goodness of creation, the goodness of dust.

This society has taught us to value human beings by external and not by internal values. This society has taught us, for example, that one USA citizen is worth 50 Haitian citizens. The modern churches of our time are the shopping centers, where people buy and sell, as if life were no more than merchandise. In shopping centers there are even Christian Churches! No wonder that Spaniard women who passed away had her ashes spread around in a mall!

134

"Remember you're dust and to dust you'll return" tells us that we are bright dust and we are going back to our Earth's womb until the resurrection!

"Remember you're dust and to dust you'll return" tells us that we are jewels of great price but not for sale, and not on clearance!

31
ARE YOU REALLY GOD'S DAUGHTER?
Mark 1:13

Ash Wednesday coincided this year with Women's International Day. March the 8th of 1856 was the day when a huge march of seamstresses fought for better salaries and working conditions having in mind the passing away of dozens of women in a sewing shop in Manhattan, NY. By 1911 March the 8th was officially accepted as International Women's Day. Our society honors that event with women's week, but the Christian church prefers to talk about women's month in order to stress the issue of women's identity, of who they are.

We are tempted to think of the Devil in very sensationalistic ways like Jim Jones expressed it, while analysing Billy Graham's speech of 1972: "He was here for two hours talking about the devil. He said, 'The devil, the devil, the devil, the devil, the devil, the devil, the devil.' He said, 'The devil here, and a little devil there.' He said, 'Everybody got a devil.' He said, 'If you're sick it's a devil. Everything's a devil. Everybody's possessed, obsessed.' . . . Why didn't God kill the devil?. . . It don't make any sense whatsoever. Bunch of fools sitting there listening to him, 50,000 people packing out a stadium, listening to that fool talking about some devil that God can't get rid of."[48] However, the Devil works in more subtle ways.

On this first Sunday in Lent we find Jesus in the wilderness, tempted by Satan during 40 days, with the apparently naive question: who are you?

If you are God's Son, order this stone to turn into bread. If you are God's Son, throw yourself down from here. The temptations have to do with Jesus' identity: who are you really? Are you really God's Son or someone else? Are you really sure you are God's Son? Satan wants to create an identity crisis to the very Jesus Christ, our Liberator!

Let's take a closer look at this matter:

I. Jesus was in the Wilderness or in the Desert for 40 Days

The desert in the Bible is a fertile land where we can find God, find ourselves and find our neighbors. In fact, the desert is considered the country of the great and courageous human souls! The 40 days remind us of the 40 years Israel was preparing in the desert for the promised land.

40 years in the desert converted a people full of fears into a people with a strong sense of who they were. Israel had to learn who there were and what their purpose in life was, as Dt. 8. 2-5 says: "Remember how YHVH our God led you on this long journey through the desert these past forty years, sending hardships to test you, so that he might know what you intended to do and whether you would obey his commands."

Actually, the book of Deuteronomy tells us about how the Israelites learned to have a clear idea of who there were. The book of Dt. deals with the identity of the entire people of Israel. The book of Deut tells us about the thoughts and the experiences of a liberated people from the dominion of Egypt.

40 years remind us also of the 40 years that our sister island of Cuba had to walk through the desert of economic isolation.

40 days also means a long period of time in the life of Jesus, in order for him to strengthen his identity.

136

II. Jesus was Tempted by Satan

It is not for nothing that Jesus' prayer included: "deliver us from evil," because Satan wants us to forget who we are.

Before Jesus started his ministry, Satan's goal was to delete the identity of Jesus Christ, the Son of God: "if you are God's Son do this... if you are God's Son, do that" because Satan knows that nobody can commit themselves to any project if they are not sure who they are.

The temptations of Jesus in the wilderness are the same Martin Luther had to face many times, when, the Reformer had to remind himself: "I can't fail because I'm a baptized son of God."

Thirdly, the tidings of great joy:

III. Jesus was Strengthened by the Dove. 11

She said: "You are my own, dear Son. I am pleased with you."

Jesus was not alone, the dove "made him go into the desert," (12) like mothers take their children to kindergarden in order for them to grow. The force of the Holy Spirit as a she, as a Dove, was the favorite way of talking among the Moravians and during March, women's month, it would be good to remember the many ways our identity comes from our dear mothers.

We learn to talk about who we are thanks to our "mother tongue." We learn to be attached to our country thanks to our "mother land" and we learn how to face the temptation of forgetting who we are, thanks to the lovely voice of the Dove: "You are my own, dear child. I am pleased with you."

In Summing up:

In March, women's month, don't forget who you are.

In the fire of 1878, 22 years after the women's march in Manhattan NY, Antiguan Mary Thomas better known as Queen Mary, Susanna Abrahmson whose nickname was Bottom Belly or Queen Mathilda and Alexina Solomon or Queen Agnes, did their part in fighting for better wage contracts, a better quality of life, more human working conditions. Queens in the Caribbean are related with the promotion of a life of plenty for everybody. Look at Queen Coziah, the Saint Thomian leader of the coal workers' strike in 1892, due to the Mexican silver crisis. They were not just nominal queens but they held power. Through the fireburn the three queens were keeping alive the traditional slave's way of social and economic protesting.

137

These women knew who they were: God's daughters worthy of a decent and full life. They were queens in the African sense. The mother was the center of the family. Women were in charge of all social activities and of feeding the family. Women brought this tradition to the Virgin Islands and here they were even more influential. A queen was chosen for every plantation or state. Queens were noticeable for their bravery, cleverness, and their sense of justice in their own states and in the others. They presided at Christmas and New Year's celebrations. They were in charge of quelling domestic and state problems among the slaves.[49] These three queen-lieutenants and ringleaders of the fireburn were captured by the French, British and United States soldiers. They were imprisoned in Denmark, but their strong sense of identity and their fight for justice took them to face the King and Queen of Denmark personally before they returned to their beloved St. Croix. Queen Mary knew who she was: a daughter of God. Still today Crucians sing her praise in one of the most popular folk songs in the Virgin Islands that strengthens the Crucians' identity as God's children.

"Kingshill Lutheran Church" is so blessed in being located on this avenue called: Queen Mary, a woman who knew who she was: God's daughter and therefore never listened to Satan: "if you are a daughter of God" do this or that. Let's never forget who we are: God's children, Jesus Christ's brothers and sisters, creatures of the motherly Dove like Queen Mary:

Queen Mary
Away you (where are you) goin' go bon (burn)
No ask'm not'n tall (don't ask me anything at all)
Just bring the match and oil
Barzen (Christiansted) jail house
away me goin' go bon.

138

32
NICODEMUS AND CIVIL DISOBEDIENCE
John 3.1-21, Numbers 21. 4-9

The night in the gospel of John means the separation of God's presence, like in Jn 9.4 says "the night is coming when no one can work" or in Jn 11.10 "if one walks during the night one stumbles." But the main meaning of the night for Nicodemus is: civil disobedience!

Some people say that this important pharisee chose the night to visit Jesus in order not to have any interruptions during his interview. Other people think that Nicodemus went during the night to see Jesus because at night is the right time to study the divine scripture. But the truth is that this Jewish leader chose the night as an act of civil and religious disobedience!

I. At Night Meant Civil Disobedience for Nicodemus

Nicodemus was well aware of the hostility of the Jewish leaders and of the official opposition to Jesus Christ. Therefore, he chose the night to visit Jesus and in doing so, Nicodemus showed that it was possible to come to the Nazarene even when those in power forbade it.

It is very revealing that several writings of the New Testament time, like the *Gospel of Nicodemus*, tell us that Nicodemus stood by Jesus before Pilate and the process of condemning our Savior. As a consequence of that daring, this Pharisee was deprived of office, and not only that, he was expelled from Jerusalem.

Nicodemus, according to this old book, was baptized by Peter and John, and when he passed away, his body was buried in a common graveyard together with Gamaliel and Stephen the martyr.

It won't surprise us then, that from Nicodemus' example follows:

II. At Night and Civil Disobedience for Yanga (1564-1612)

Yanga, "The Black King", according to some historians was a prince from what is currently the Ivory Coast. Other scholars are of the opinion that he used to belong to the Yanga Bara tribe from the Nile River region. He was made a slave and taken to Mexico, where he ran away and lived in the mountains for 30 years. He survived by planting cotton, corn, beans, hot pepper, squash, sugar cane, tobacco and vegetables. At the beginning of the 16th century God sent the Afro-Mexican Yanga to liberate his people in Orizaba, Veracruz valley. By 1608 the Veracruz town "San Lorenzo de los negros" also known as "San Lorenzo de Cerralvo" changed its name to "Yanga", in honor of its liberator. In 1631 this town conquered the official recognition of "the First Free Town of America." In the 21st century Veracruz still celebrates the feast in memory of Yanga, the civil disobedient runaway who stood on the side of his suffering people. During Easter of 1612 he was betrayed and killed but Yanga´s name since 1608 has been associated with "the First City for Free Blacks in the Americas."[50]

III. At Night and Civil Disobedience for Zumbi Dos Palmares (1655-1695)

140

Zumbi was born in the Black Republic of Palmares, Brazil in 1655. He was taken prisoner as a newborn baby and given to Father Antonio Melo of Porto Calvo, a Portugues priest, who baptized the child as Francisco. By the age of 10 he could read Latin and Portuguese very well, as he played the acholite role. At the age of 15 Francisco ran away to his birthplace of Palmares where two years later he became the chief and changed his name to Zumbi, meaning "God of war." Zumbi defended his people from the constant attacks of the Dutch and Portuguese colonialists. Palmares was a city of refuge for civil disobedients for amost a century, building up a completely new society, with a new economy, a new language, a new religion and a new sense of family ties.[51]

IV. At Night Meant Civil Disobedience for M L King

The great champion of the civil rights movement knew the story of his people and knew the story of the person in whm his people found inspiration: that is, Nicodemus, besides Gandhi and Henry David Thoreau.

The African American community looked upon Nicodemus as a symbol of "obeying God before Human Beings" (Acts 5.19). Consequently, they were willing to risk their safety and their very lives to come to Jesus. During the time of slavery, hey held clandestine religious gatherings at night. And in a clandestine way, they were able to preserve their names, their way of eating, of dressing, of celebrating, of walking, of greeting, of loving, of sharing, of singing, of dancing, of believing, of laughing. In a clandestine way, they kept their ientity alive.

"Kingshill Lutheran Church" started worshiping during the afternoons from 1916, but it was because this church had to share their pastor with the Lutheran church at Frederiksted.

At night, in clandestine meetings, ML King trained his people by means of drama, how to endure the non-violent protest in the midst of the police brutality. He used to preach this way: "We are called to play the Good Samaritan on life's roadside...one day the whole Jericho road must be transfomed so that men and women will not be beaten and robbed as they make their journey through life. True compassion is more than flinging a coin to a beggar; it understands that an edifice which produces beggars needs restructuring."[52]

Finally, this Nicodemus night points to Jesus' night:

141

V. At Night Meant Civil Disobedience for Jesus Christ

Lent means a season for preparing ourselves for Easter. Therefore, this nocturnal clandestine conversation of Jesus with Nicodemus reminds us of the last Supper of our Savior. That was a clandestine Supper. Many security measures where involved. The apostles in charge of setting up thetable had to follow a man carrying a water container like a woman, etc. Jesus had to use a code language in order to find his way around: the code to get a donkey on his trip to Jerusalem was: "the Lord needs it." (Lk19.31) Or take the known words for Judas, the apostle who revealed the clandestine meeting: "Be quick about it." (Mt 26.50)

In Conclusion

Let us celebrate this 2nd Sunday of Lent, keeping in mind that the unjust laws and attitudes that tried to separate Nicodemus, Yanga, Zumbi, ML King, and Jesus himself from their caring God and their dear people, is not going to last forever.

What else can we say about the list of African-Americans, obedient to the gospel? We ran out of time to talk about Colombian Reina Leonor (1633); Central American Bayano (16th century) Jamaican Cudjoe (Leeward, 17th-18th centuries) Haitian Cécile Fatiman the revolutionary woman of 1791 and Toussaint L'ouverture (1743-1803); Venezuelan Miguel Negro (1500) and Domingo Bioho (16th-17th centuries); Ecuatorian Alonso de Illescas (1528-1585); Peruvian Bonifacio (17th century); Argentinian Falucho (Antonio Ruiz, -1824); Mexican José María Morelos y Pavón born of an African-Mexican mother (1765-1815), Grenadian Julien Fédon (1795), Rosa Parks and the Montgomery bus boycott, Kaála from Surinam, and so forth.

In the 19th century God sent Buddho to liberate his West Indies people. In the 20th century Rothschild Francis, "Our Great Liberator" was the champion of the Virgin Islands' self determination.

Civil laws that denied God's love are subject to be disobeyed. Nicodemus, Yanga, Zumbi, M.L. King, and Jesus tell us so.

142

33

THE GOD WHO FORGIVES ECONOMIC DEBTS
Luke 15.11-32

The Moravians had very difficult times with the landowners because they didn't limit themselves to sharing the Gospel. They also taught the slaves to read and write. I don't know when and how, but slaves eventually learned Math! Yes, they learned to add and subtract, and that was a revolutionary action. After the end of slavery, the Math of the landowners said: "3 times 7 is 65; here you are 5 bucks change and we are even!" When the liberated slaves learned to add and subtract, they had quite a different mathematics, like the Afro-American protest song states:

Our Father who is in heaven

White man owe me eleven and pay me seven,

Thy Kingdom come, thy will be done,

And if I hadn't took that,

I wouldn't had none.

Well, the gospel of this morning talks about math. Jesus draws two pictures of God: God as a book keeper and the God who forgives economic debts.

First:

I. God as a book keeper

In the parable of the Prodigal Son we first meet a father and mother, could he be a widower? He raised two children and all of a sudden the younger one is requesting the part of his inheritance. The younger brother went ahead and lost all his goodies in the twinkling of an eye. In his poverty and misery he decides to go back to his home. But it won't be easy, since his older brother has been keeping good track of the family money book.

Jesus again has the pharisees and scribes on the spot. That means that Jesus is denouncing the way top church leaders understand God. The pharisees and scribes are like the older son. They have the strong belief that God is like a book keeper who doesn't forgive and forget economic debts. The older brother refuses to participate in his father's loving forgiveness of his younger brother. The older brother condemns his father's open arms to all, especially to the people that stink, the poor, the miserable, like his younger brother.

The older brother, like the Pharisees and scribes, worships a God who does a financial balance very often to remind us that we are in debt. The God that, like the IRS (Internal Revenue Service), doesn't forgive economic debts. Economy comes from a Greek word: oikos, which means house. The older brother understands economy not like the caring administration of the house, but like the way of accumulating wealth. That is why he just doesn't get what his father is doing.

The culinary novel *Like Water for Chocolate*, is a femenine narrative of Goddess as a book keeper. Mamá Elena was a frustrated mother who wasn't allowed to marry José Treviño, a son of a beautiful Afro-Mexican, due to his blackness. Mamá Elena oriented her bitterness especially toward her youngest daughter Tita, who ended up rebeling in radical ways. The authoritarian mother decided to send her daughter to a mental hospital across the Mexican border. Chencha, the cook and maid, found her way to pay Tita a visit and heal her with delicious dishes, but on her way back had to invent a white lie in order to justify her absense: "She would tell Mama Elena that she'd been passing through Eagle Pass and had seen a beggar

144

on the street-corner, dressed in filthy, tattered clothes. Moved by pity, she had gone over to give her a coin and had been shocked at the discovery that the beggar was Tita. She had escaped from the lunatic asylum and was roaming the world to pay for the crime of having insulted her mother. Chencha had invited her to come back home, but Tita had refused. She didn't feel she deserved to return and live with such a good mother, and she had asked Chencha to please tell her mother that she loved her dearly and would never forget how much she had always done for her, and she promised that as soon as she became an honest woman she would return to be with her mother and give all the love and respect that Mama Elena deserved."[53] The true story is that Tita was recovering in the nice Doctor's family home, and that the last place she would like to go was to her inflexible book keeper mother.

Second:

II. The God who forgives economic debts

The homeless, jobless, friendless, credit cardless, the bankrupt younger brother is going home. He has prepared his speech to deliver to his father. He is getting close to home and is still brushing up and organizing his ideas. But, by the time he realizes it, he is in his father's warm arms.

According to Jesus the father in this parable is the best portrait of God. God is the one who forgives economic debts. God is hospitable to the poor, the forsaken, the lost, the dying people. God doesn't go by the book! God breaks every rule of what appears to be proper household management.

The rules he was supposed to follow were clear: He should have waited at his home for his sinning son, seated in his wing-backed chair surrounded by all the symbols of his paternal authority. He should have received a formal apology from his son. He should have clothed his son with labor clothes, and he should have received his son as a worker. But the father breaks all the rules, he just doesn't follow the book, he is not a book keeper!

The father rushes to embrace the pig-smelling, dirt-caked child. He forgives the economic debts even before his son finishes his apology. The father doesn't say: "you see, I told you, but you never listen to me!" The father dresses his son with a royal suit. The father empoweres his son by giving him his own ring. The father orders a luxurious meal, because this is a real celebration. In a few words, the father represents the God who breaks all the rules. The God who forgives economic debts.

You may very well argue: "hey pastor, the father forgives money debts because he is his son." Well, I would answer you, "that's right, but the older brother knew mathematics and he knew the rules of those times, and the right thing to do was just to hire his younger brother as a servant. That was the right thing to do."

To put it more simply:

This is the 4th Sunday in Lent. Lent is a season where we Christians have to remember that our God is a God who forgives economic debts!

Every Sunday I enjoy singing the Lord's Prayer calypso style, because you don't recite: "forgive us our trespasses as we forgive those who trespass against us." No, you say it the right way: "forgive us our debts as we forgive our debtors." Still more, by debts you mean: financial debts, economic debts. Sister Myra Ballantine put it so well in one of her poems:

Tell me all about this life,
and the world in which we live.
The many people with their wealth,
who do not care to give?

We live in a society that has the color of the money where you are valued by what you have. We live in a world of book keepers who don't forgive a single dollar. And not only that, our way of doing business is as if we don't know Math, like in slavery times.

But the liberating news is that our God is a God who breaks all the rules, a God who doesn't go by the book like Mama Elena. A God who is building a new household. A God who is building a new economy that gives to all, that promotes access to abundant life for all, including the poor people like the prodigal son.

The gospel is not a set of obligations to keep. The gospel is a style of life to follow, and in the Kingdom of God we are responsible for the homeless and miserable people like the prodigal son.

The kingdom of God doesn't follow the mathematics of the older brother, but the mathematics of the generous God who forgives economic debts!

147

34
THE FOR-GIVING GOD
Luke 13.1-9

Like a week ago, Lionel Tate, the African-American 14 year-old boy, was judged as an adult for killing Eunick, two years ago, while they were imitating the catch wrestling. Lionel Tate is going to spend his entire life in an adult prison without any guaranty of safety. Amnesty International already denounced this violation of the international principle of not judging people under 18 as an adult.

A month ago president Bush did his first presidential visit overseas in order to buy electricity for California. He went to the Mexican president's ranch. The media spent a good deal of time figuring out how to take pictures of both presidents since Bush is noticeably shorter in comparison with the very tall Mexican President. Pictures were taken while riding horses, and in other ways to avoid Bush appearing shorter than the Mexican Vicente Fox.

This is because our society has taught us that some people are superior to others, that there is such a thing as biological inferiority. Have you heard of an Euro-American boy being sentenced to life imprisonment? Is it possible for a greaser Mexican to appear taller than President Bush? All of this has to do with the doctrine of temporal retribution.

Let me explain it by means of drawing two images of God: the God of punishment and the for-giving God.

First:

I. The God of Punishment
Luke mentions two historical events we don't know: when Pilate

killed some Galileans while there were offering sacrifices to God, and also mentions the 18 people who were killed in Siloam when a tower fell on them. According to the doctrine of retribution, if those people were killed in that way, it was because they committed some kind of sin. But Jesus completely disagreed with that interpretation.

Jesus' ministry included to take care of the "blonds" uuppss! I mean, to take care of the "blinds." For example, in John 9.18 Jesus cured a man who was blind since his birth. The natural question at that time was: since he is a blind person, who committed sin? He himself or his parents? But in healing him, Jesus answered that none of them committed sin, that the doctrine of temporal retribution is wrong.

The retribution doctrine says that disease, misfortune, poverty are the result of sin. Therefore, the suffering people who face their harsh life are also burdened by a painful sense of guilt. In other words, the victims of illness, of poverty, of death, are besides that, victimized with guilt. This crime is called the victimization of the victim.

The retribution doctrine can be located as far back as the times of the book of Job. His friends, the theologians, insist on justifying the God of punishment and insist on condemning Job, following the formula: sickness and poverty equals a sinner. But Jesus completely rejects that formula.

In the mid 19th century there was a Danish Lutheran pastor, whose last name Kierkegaard means the cemetery of the church, like our micro cemetery of Kingshill! His fiancé came to St. Croix as a governess of the West Indies when she married the Governor. Kierkegaard reflected on the sinful misfortunes of this oppressive doctrine of temporal retribution, which makes the suffering people the very ones responsible for their sufferings. According to this Danish Lutheran, to link sin with sickness and poverty is in fact a sinful act, as to judge by the external. He said:

"if someone is a cripple or is deformed or has an unfavorable

149

appearance, then to judge that he is an evil person, so that he amounts to nothing or is down and out, then to judge that he is a bad person, what an exquisitely contrived kind of cruel enjoyment to want to feel one's own righteousness in relation to someone who is suffering by explaining his suffering as God's punishment upon him."[54]

Now let's go to our second point:

II. The Patient, Trusting God

Jesus begins rejecting the doctrine of temporal retribution. For Jesus there is no connection between having misfortunes and being a sinner. There is no connection between being killed by human causes like Pilate, or being killed by natural causes like the fall of the tower of Siloam, and being a sinner.

Jesus is trying to make us understand that this world is not a world of justice. That if some people died —either by human causes like Pilate, or by natural disasters like the earthquake of India— that doesn't mean that they deserved that death. All that takes place in this world is not God's will. God shares the rain for good and evil people. God shares his sun for good and evil people. God is not a God of punishment and wrath, like the God of many TV evangelists and preachers who, it seems to me, are angry the whole time.

Jesus brings to us a new image of God. God is not the God of punishment but the for-giving God, as Jesus illustrates in the parable of the unfruitful fig tree.

Jesus frees us from passivity: "Oh there is nothing we can do." Jesus frees us from fate: "If people are killed either by the modern Pilates or by modern natural causes like in El Salvador, it is due to the sin those folks committed." No, no. Jesus is plunging us to find the real causes of being killed, of being sick, of suffering poverty, in order to look for a solution.

And part of the solution is to change the image of the God of punishment to the patient and trusting God.

Instead of wasting our time figuring out what kind of sin people have committed when they have to face death, illness, poverty, Jesus invites us to lie fruitful lives. And in doing so, year after year, Lenten after Lenten, our God is like the vineyard farmer who digs around, who puts fertilizer, who waters our lives in order to become fruitful lives. An African American song put it well:

Children, we shall be free
when the Lord shall ppear.
Give ease to the sick, give sight to the blind
enable the cripple to walk;
He'll raise the dead from under the earth,
and give them permission to talk.

Now let me piggyback to the two stories of the beginning.

John D. Rockefeller had the conviction that nature rewards the fittest and punishes the useless.

The God of punishment of the doctrine of temporal retribution tells us that colored people like the boy Lionel Tate and President Vicente Fox are getting what they deserve, one life imprisonment, the other not to be taller than Bush. The God of punishment punishes only some people, and praises only some people. Believe it or not, people still are of the idea that we, people of dark skin are more suitable for hard work, for the sugar cane cutting, for the hot tropical sun labor, etc. But that's not true. Edson Arantes do Nascimento, Pelé, the Afro-Brazilian soccer player king, demonstrated that, when in the midst of the snow fromSweden he played as well as in his tropical country, getting first place in the wrld wide championship.

151

Our sinful society has organized the world according to the punishing God of the doctrine of temporal retribution. But the liberating news is that the for-giving God says quite a different thing. Our God is waiting for everybody to be fruitful. There is no room in God's house for sterile fig trees.

There are billions of people that died either by human or natural causes and society still punishes them with guilt! There are thousands of people whose style of life is: "fun and sun", "no rum, no fun" "golden sun and gentle breeze" and still, society praises them! They sure live unfruitful lives!

According to Presiden Clinton's report right now there are 1.3 billion people whose daily income is one dollar. The World Bank just informed us that currently there are 2.3 billion people whose daily income is two dollars. And it happens to be that the vast majority of these people belong to the Southern countries.

According to Noam Chomsky, 230 families own 80% of the world's wealth.

You Virgin Islanders are very cautious with water. In fact, the majority of you depend almost entirely on rainy water. Whereas the Northern countries spend more than a gallon every day just for brushing their teeth, and an average of 92 gallons (300 to 400 liters) of water per person on a daily basis. The first thing Columbus was looking for in St. Croix on November 14, 1493, was fresh water. But since the industrial Revolution, water has been considered just another detergent. At least from 1841 to 1867 St. Thomas was widely known as the best port of water supply for all the ships that crossed the Caribbean! It is not for nothing that currently there is a scarcity of water on the Island. Water has lost its enchantment, the industries use 5 to 10 times more water than domestic needs.

Our for-giving God is granting his world one more year, God is going to dig around and to put some fertilizer in his creatures, in order for them to repent and for them to become fruitful. Our patient and trusting God wants for everybody to live fruitful lives! God still trusts us! God still waits for us!

152

35
THE RESHAPING OF SOCIETY
Matthew 17.1-9

One candidate to the ministry, who was known for inventing what he did not know, heard the following question on his ordination examination: "What did John the Baptist say to Jesus when he came in order to be baptized?" He almost immediately answered: "What John the Baptist said to Jesus was: remember you are God's son, you better behave as such."[55]

What that candidate and many of us often forget is the «messianic secret»: it means that Jesus was a mystery for he himself. Jesus asks his disciples about his own identity, about his own secret. It was not a puzzle, it was the most honest of all questions. The candidate to be ordained never ever doubted; but Jesus was as unsure of himself as any of us in need of feedback. Jesus Christ needed badly to hear the first confession of faith of the Christian church, that of Martha (Jn 11.27): "Yes, Savior, I do believe that you are the Messiah, the Son of God, who was to come into the world." Jesus needed to hear the messianic secret when Peter was inspired to say (Lk 9.20): "You are God's Messiah." When John baptized Jesus it was so energetic for our Savior to see the Dove and to hear God's voice as it was registered in Psalm 2.7, (Lk 3.22): "You are my own dear Son. I am pleased with you."

And here we are, at the top of the transfiguration mountain, experiencing God's confirmation of Jesus as the Son of God and dissipating his Son's doubts. (Lk 9.35) The words "This is my Son,

Whom I have chosen —listen to him" then, remit us to the realm of the Spirit:

I. The Contemplative Life

Contemplation means to go into the temple. And Jesus himself was a being in need of seeing God's glory, of having this transfigurating experience in order to strengthen his own identity as the Son of God.

No wonder we as human beings have to be in touch with the realm of the Spirit. The history of God's people is full of examples: Moses and the burning bush; Elijah and the chariots of fire (2 Kings, 1.2); Deborah and her palm tree where she had revelations (Judges 4.5); (2 Kings 22.14) Huldah and her prophecies; (1.1) Ezequiel and his vision of the open sky; (6.14) Isaiah and his mystical experience in the temple; Paul and the third heaven (2 Cor 12.2); John and the open door to heaven (Rev 4.1).

To be Christian is to have had a transfiguration experience: "Savior, how good it is that we are here! We will make three tents, one for you, one for Moses, and one for Elijah." But, there is always the temptation of not wanting to return to our worldly reality. There is always the risk of fleeing to an otherworldly religion which prefers to see God in power, in wisdom, in happiness, in prestige.

But the criteria for an authentic Christian rapturous experience is to go down from the mountain through:

II. The Committed Life

154

The transfigured Jesus even during that time on top of the hill, was not able to forget his beloved everyday world: he was talking about his imminent death in Jerusalem. He was thinking of all his pending task of reshaping society. The theology of the cross never forgets to see God in suffering, in weakness, in folly.

Moses' shining face (Ex 34.29) felt good with God at the top of

Mount Sinai. Nevertheless, he had to go down and transfigure the ugly form of his people, organization, laws, guidance, with manna.

Elijah (1 Kings 19.12) felt good with the soft whisper of God's voice. Nonetheless, he had to reshape his people, he had to restore the true worship against the prophets of Baal. He had to hurry up and feed the dying widow and her son in Zarephath. (1 Kings 17.10-16)

Currently we have many examples of the spiritual ecstasy of Christian mystics: Helder Camara, Dorothee Soelle, Thomas Merton, Simone Weil, Pedro Casaldáliga. Those women and men have experienced the Transfiguration of Jesus, but, at the same time they have promoted the recreation of society.

To make the story short:

Once the transfiguration of Jesus was over, the disciples kept quiet about all this.

They needed time to digest the enraptured vision. They also needed a break to plan their program of reshaping the world. We, as well, need to experience, first hand, the glory of God in order to be agents of transfiguring society: "Your will be done on earth, as it is in heaven."

Martin Luther King, whose birthday was on January the 18th, was a contemplating man who in his very last sermon insisted on transfiguring his society:

"Tell everybody I was a mayor drum, but a mayor drum for justice. Never ever mention I won the Noble Peace Prize; that is completely irrelevant. I would like somebody to mention during the day of my burial that Martin Luther King tried to give his life serving the humble people. On that day I would like somebody to mention that Martin Luther King tried to love somebody. If any of you are around when I pass away, I would like for you to mention that Martin Luther King does not want a big funeral."[56]

155

Luther King saw the glory of Jesus but he never forgot to see and to challenge the ugly side of society.

Many "Crucians", tourists and foreigners who live here have for sure contemplated the glory of God in this paradisiac Island. But how many are committed to transfiguring this country according to the Kingdom of God? The shape of St. Croix has changed a lot: Currently the Government is thinking of running an airline in order to accelerate tourism, because the Island is associated with vacation time, pretty soon with gambling in the casino, duty free shops, and leisure lives. Yesterday the shape of St. Croix was related to the sugar plantations and the hard work. If a pastor wanted to visit a worker it had to be either before 5.30 a.m. or after 6.00 p.m. The day of tomorrow we can foresee a community of Crucians, Dominicans, Puertorricans, and Northatlantic citizens living together. We, as Luther King, have the vision that this transfiguration of the Island will take place with justice and peace, remembering that in God's Kingdom there is room for everybody.

We as Christians should question our identity and not be so sure of ourselves like that imprudent candidate to the ministry. We must, without rush yet without delay, be an illuminated or visionary people, committed to the reshaping of the world.

156

36
WE BE JAMMIN!
2 Samuel 6.16-23; Matthew 21.1-11

Alexander the Great (356-323 b.c.e.) was the King of Macedonia who during his last 10 years of life conquered most of the world known to antiquity: Persia, Tyre, Egypt, Babylon, etc. Every time he entered into a conquered city, he was received with all the honor and glory. Alexander the Great knew what a triumphal entry meant.

This "Palm Sunday" we find Jesus entering Jerusalem. Jesus is not riding a war horse, He is not carrying a sword, nor wearing a military uniform. This is actually more an anti-triumphal entry!

The triumphal entry of Alexander the Great and the anti-triumphal entry of Jesus into Jerusalem in fact, reminds us of two ways in which Christians used to worship God: "the decently and orderly time!" And the "rocking, shouting, singing jammin time!"

First:

I. The Decently and Orderly Time

The high churches think of God in terms of an earthly emperor like Alexander the Great, almighty and everlasting!

For example, a Native American theologian[57] warns us about the worshiping of God from up on high. This Sioux theologian mentions when President Nixon visited the University of Tennessee in 1970 to address Billy Graham's revival meeting. As Nixon was seated awaiting Graham's introduction, a choir of 5,500 voices sang: "How

Great Thou Art." Now, this Native American raises the question: "to which 'thou' was the choir trumpeting? To Alexander the Great or to Jesus?

"Hosana to David's Son" says Matthew 21.9 "God bless him who comes in the name of the King." That connects us with 2 Samuel 6.16-23, that mentions King David's entry into Jerusalem.

Now, in David's time the standard version of worshiping God was according to the Levite's Book of Worship. It was centered on the priest. Since the sacrifices played a central role and only the Levites were authorized to perform them, people were mere spectators.

But the good news is that David introduces a new way of worshiping God.[58]

And that takes us to our second point:

II. Rocking, Shouting, Singing Jammin time!

King David abandoned the priest-centered, highly elaborate and stiff worshiping of God according to the Levites, decently and orderly.

At the gates of Jerusalem, David introduces a popular worship based on processions, singing and dancing psalms, prayers and shouting. David involves all people and not only the priests, in joyfully worshiping God, or in what is known as the low liturgy. Michal his wife didn't change to the low liturgy. She remained inside looking out from a window the way David was dancing and jumping with light clothes, mingling with the poor people. First thing she said to David when he got inside was something like: "stop jammin with that short skirt!

158

This Palm Sunday it is precisely what is taking place. Jesus is taking his distance from the highly professional, decently and orderly, Scribes and Pharisees - centered worshiping of God in the temple of Jerusalem. Instead of that, Jesus is recuperating the popular way of worshiping like King David. On Palm Sunday it was not Michal but the Pharisees the ones who wanted to stop the noisy and emotional worshiping: "command your disciples to be quiet" but Jesus rebuked them: "I tell you that if they keep quiet, the stones themselves will start shouting."

According to Luke 19.37 this noisy and highly emotional worshiping was led by the crowd, but this crowd was integrated by Jesus' disciples who followed him, who were healed and fed, who were enrolled in following Jesus in true discipleship taking their cross every day. This crowd was not the one of Jerusalem who on the next Friday would cry "crucify Him, crucify Him."

In addition, our Palm Sunday text tells us that people from Jerusalem not even knew Jesus: "Who is he?" they asked. "He is Jesus the prophet from Nazareth in Galilee" was the answer. So what! No big deal for the Jerusalem citizens since Galileans were second or third class citizens! Anyhow, Jesus and the crowd of his disciples kept on singing, shouting, walking and dancing like David at the gates of Jerusalem.

A final statement:

Sisters and brothers from the US Virgin Islands and from all over the places where you're listening to this broadcasting worship, just allow me to mention the following.

As time went by, Christian churches went back to the Levite style of worshiping, of the priest - centered churches. The good thing is that in the 16th century Martin Luther recuperated the way of worshiping God that took place at the gates of Jerusalem in David's and Jesus' time.

159

Martin Luther was a musician, a composer and an emotional Christian. He himself used to sing in parties and dances in order to support his studies. Our organist, brother Shelton Arthur Shulterbrandt, as he plays in a band, is just following Luther's steps! Among other aspects of the Reformation of the 16th century was the reform from the high to the popular way of worshiping. Martin Luther took popular melodies from the parties in society and introduced them to the church, like the melody of "Almighty Fortress is our God". Luther rejected the "decently and orderly liturgy," and prefered the "rocking, shouting, singing, jammin time".

At the beginning of the 21st century, the Lutheran church in the Virgin Islands is more at home with the way of worshiping at Jerusalem's gates: Rocking, shouting, singing, jammin time! Please don't listen to Michal's command "stop jammin with that short skirt!" Please don't listen to the modern Pharisees' command: "tell your disciples to be quiet." All people are to be empowered, especially the physically challenged, the Galileans, that is, our sisters and brothers from the other Caribbean islands, the outsiders, the despised, the poor. Let's worship God with the flavor of Quadrille, Quaile Bay, soca, calypso, reggae, merengue, salsa, plena, bomba, gospel music.

Hey, all of you, guess what: "We be jammin!"

160

37
THE RESURRECTION FROM BELOW
Luke 24.1-12

From the very beginning, the Christian church used to have vigils. Chances are that they were inspired by the fact that Jesus had the discipline of praying during the night. Or maybe due to the parable of the ten watching virgins. Or perhaps because of persecution, the first Christians had to meet at night in clandestine reunions.

The Lutheran churches of the Virgin Islands keep alive the Easter Vigil as they begin on Saturday after the Sun sets. The Lutheran churches of Puerto Rico prefer instead, to wake up early on Sunday, before the Sun rises in order to celebrate Jesus Christ's resurrection. The first Christians commemorated the resurrection of Jesus every week. As time went by Easter was honored just once a year. The vigils then were limited mainly to Easter and Pentecost, but the Anglican Book of Worship still recommends 16 vigils during the year!

Anyhow, let us focus our attention on what we have been waiting for during the whole long year, and on what Kingshill has been waiting for 3 years: Easter Vigil. Especially since St. Croix's Easter Vigil tradition was first hosted at Kingshill, and pastor William Montgomery, a classmate of pastor Wakefield, was the pioneer.

There are two ways of approaching Jesus Christ's Resurrection: from above and from below. The Resurrection from above has to do with a triumphalistic, successful, everything under control, Hollywood style of portraying almighty and majestic Jesus Christ back to business! Seated at the right hand of the Father way up on high. But we prefer to celebrate the Resurrection of Jesus Christ from below: from the point of view of the defeated, the failures, the despised. In order to illustrate that, I propose two points: the resurrection of creation and the resurrection of women.

First:

I. The Resurrection of Creation

"Very early on the eighth day the women went to the tomb," says our Easter vigil story. When God created the universe he made it in 6 days and rested on the seventh. It means that the eighth day, the day of Jesus Christ's resurrection points to the beginning of the new creation. Not surprisingly the first Christians baptized the eighth day as Resurrection Day! And they *did* celebrate it every week!

Due to the influence of Greek philosophy, the earth and creation in general have been seen as evil, as so low and despicable. What matters, according to the Greeks, is the soul, the spirit, the mind; the material world is not worthy, creation is to be dominated, the Earth is to be exploited.

However, Jesus' resurrection involves the salvation of the whole creation. The resurrection of Jesus' body means the resurrection of dust from the Earth, it means the resurrection of the Earth itself! The Christian church of the first centuries understood it very well. It is not for nothing that the festival of Easter coincides with the festival of spring. "The springtime of nature was interpreted as the symbol of the eternal springtime of the new creation of all things. This is the meaning of Easter eggs, too! Nor is it by chance that the Christian feast of Pentecost coincides with the beginning of summer. The greening and flowering of nature was seen as a symbol of the eternal quickening of the whole creation in the breath of the divine Spirit."[59]

It is not by accident that the first baptismal fountains had an octagonal shape. 7 sides remembered the 7 days of creation and

162

the 8th side remembered the beginning of the new creation. Therefore, the children who were baptized already share the power of the new creation and all of us who this evening renewed our baptismal vows, share the power of the new creation!

The resurrection from below honors the material world. This resurrection from below was very well understood by St. Martin de Porres. He was an Afro-Peruvian who lived by the end of 16th century and the beginning of the 17th, but was canonized until 1962, and by the way, he was the first African-South American saint of the long, long calendar of saints. It took almost 450 years to canonize this Afro-Peruvian because he sided with the people from below and also because he used to give the holy Eucharist to animals! Well, the eighth day, Resurrection day tells us precisely about that, about the new creation, the resurrection of creation, the resurrection from below! Jesus Christ also gave his blood for mangus, for cows, for the higbiscus, for the guavaberry tree, for your national symbols of Bananaquit birth and Cedar Flower. Jesus Christ's resurrection involves the whole creation, because creation is not something bad, as the Greeks used to think. If God is good all the time, and if God created everything, and if God Godself was incarnated and resurrected in a human body, then creation is good!

Jesus Christ's resurrection viewed from below, involves stopping the bombarding of Vieques. It involves stopping the cruises's terrible pollution of our seas and ports. It involves participating in the Kioto agreement of cleaning our environment. USA represents 4% of the world population but USA represents 25 % of the world pollution.

Now, let us go to our second point:

II. The Resurrection of Women

"Very early on the eighth day the women went to the tomb," says our Easter vigil story. The leader was, of course, Mary of Magdalene, better known as the *Apostola apostolorum* which means, the apostle to the apostles, the 1st Christian, the 1st witness of the resurrection, the 1st preacher of the resurrection, the 1st teacher of the apostles, one of the first ladies who supported Jesus. Since our lectionary repeats her story tomorrow Sunday, we had better concentrate on the women who went to the tomb.

About this group of women says verse 11 "the apostles didn't believe them." The apostles didn't believe them simply because women's declarations in general didn't count in Jesus' time. Tonight we don't have to go to the painful endless list of examples of how women were denied a place of honor and dignity.

Suffice it to say that yesterday and today society and unfortunately many times the Christian church too, just don't believe people who are declared inferior. Take a look for example at what happened last Saturday with the killing of 19-year-old Timothy Thomas. Since 1995 15 African-American disarmed people have been killed "accidentally" by the police brutality of Cincinnati. Cincinnati declared a kind of tridum, three days of curfew in order not to add more people to the 82 arrested and more than 70 injured. Take for example what happened on the Island of Hainan, China. Bush never asked for forgiveness because he considers Asians biologically inferior. Take for instance what happens on the USA - Mexico border where at least one person is killed every day even by a bullet or by hunger and thirst.

Women were considered nobodies. But Jesus Christ's resurrection reminds us that in his kingdom there are not nobodies, that in his Kingdom the rule is "women first, children first, outcast first, the dregs of society first, the people from below first!"

On Resurrection day women went to the tomb. But during his whole ministry and also on Resurrection day Jesus Christ resurrected women to a place of honor and dignity.

This Easter Vigil 2001 let us honor and recognize all Virgin Islands women who, like the women of our Easter story, have been so

164

courageous in witnessing Jesus Christ's resurrection. Women who have been our teachers, our chaplains, our inspiration, our spiritual mothers.

We can think of Sister Emma Francis, the first African-American deaconess in the Lutheran Church in the United States. She was born inSt. Kitts (1875). As a clever woman she was able, in a very imaginative way, to get her education as a school teacher in Antigua. On a "Good Friday" that WestIndian girl arrived inHamburg,Germany to be trained as a nurse and as a deaconess. Emma Francis ministered inPuerto Rico and in th States but her heart and her main ministry took place in Queen Louise Home for Children in Fredericksted,St. Croix, and she did everything without a salary!

We can think of Sister ThelmaYoungblood, the first deaconess of the Virgin Islands and of the Caribbean Synod. She got her theological training in the Motherhouse of Deaconesses in Philadelphia. She ministered and planted the first and second African-American Lutheran churches i Denver and Toledo, Ohio, together with her husband, pastor Allen G Youngblood. She continued being a co-pastor at Holy Trinity and after her husband's passing away, Siste Youngblood has ben a pastor for Kingshill, ordained by heavenly authorities. And she has done everything without a salary!

We can also think of lay women who have served the altar: From "Christus Victor" we thank God this Easter vigil for commited, valiant women like Corlis Nathaniel, like Mrs. Gabriel Williams and like Ms. Evelyn Crittenden.

From "Holy Trinity" we honor the faithfulness and Christian service of Ms. Asta James, of Ms. Doris Brown, of Ms. Gertrude Arnold.

From "Lord God of Sabaoth" we praise the Lord for strong examples of dedication of women like Ms. Beatriz Immanuel, of Ms. Benjamin, of Ms.Ruth Beagles.

From "Kingshill" we recognize with deep gratitude the Christian witnessing ofMs. Chi Thomas, of Ms. Emma Grant, ofMs. Dolorita Davis, of Ms. Beryl Santos.

"Very early on the eighth day the women went to the tomb."

And there at the tomb they were the first to confess: "Christ is risen, He is risen indeed!"

Jesus, the carpenter, the bricklayer, the mason, the fisherman, the cook, the artisan from Nazareth of Galilee, the political prisioner who was condemned to the death penalty is risen! said the women.

Pilate, the Saducees, the Pharisees, the Scribes, the executioners just couldn't get rid of him, because He is risen! said the women. What these women are preaching makes a lot of sense to all the movements that fight for a more just society, to all the people who invest their hearts and lives for a more humane world, to all the organizations involved in enviromental struggles since: Christ is Risen! He is risen indeed!

38
IRIE!
John 20.19

"Peace be with you" was the way Christians greeted each other 2,000 years ago. The equivalent of today is the Rasta Fari: "Irie!" Meaning "may you be well," "have a good day," "Be happy," "God bless you."

In Jesus' time people greeted each other with a kiss, including kissing among men: we remember Judas' famous kissing of Jesus. Our country fellows from Alaska, before the arrival of TV, greeted each other by rubbing their noses. Today we greet each other with a hug to show affection, although in Mexico the origin of the hug was to be sure that the other person didn't carry a weapon! I've seen the very original ways Crucians greet each other with their hands, but the most important greeting is "Irie!"

In the Virgin Islands when some one greets you with the question: "How're you doing?" the answer is "A dé," which means "nothing worse. " Then one is supposed to celebrate: "Oh, You dé de!", meaning "Oh, you're not too bad!"

The first Christians used to say hello and good-by with the same expression: "peace be with you," which is close to our "Irie!" The first Christians wanted for everybody to experience and to live a life of plenty!

Let us see then what is the real meaning of "Irie."

I. For Greeks and Romans, Peace was the Absence of War.
They used to say: *Si vis pacem, para bellum* (if you wish peace,

prepare for war). For the Roman empire too, peace (*Pax*), was achieved thanks to the legions of the army who captured, tortured and killed Jesus Christ.

This understanding of peace is the same as the one the seven countries of the seven flags had when they ruled the Virgin Islands. They wanted to preserve order or peace, by means of silencing and repressing the voices of Buddoe, of the Queens of the fireburn, of D. Hamilton Jackson who was considered public enemy number one, and one of the most dangerous persons in the 20th century from the viewpoint of the planters, of Rothschild Francis, the "Great Liberator."

Still today, many people continue believing that, in order to have peace they have to be involved in war. Currently the world spends 800 billion dollars each year on weapons in order to reach peace. Our neighbor island of Vieques is the closest example of the Greek and Roman idea of pursuing peace through war.

II. For Pious Christians Peace has to do with an Inner Feeling.

St. Augustine, influenced by the stoic philosophy (Varro), understood peace as to be still and quiet, to develop an internal control in order to reach (*ataraxia*) inner tranquility.

Today many Christians and non Christians still run the risk of understanding peace as an inner feeling which, sooner or later, becomes insensitive toward the suffering of our neighbors. For many people peace means a nice relationship between my soul and God and that's it.

This mellifluous way of understanding peace was severely criticized by St. James 2.15: "Suppose there are brothers or sisters who need clothes and don't have enough to eat. What good is there in your greeting them: 'peace be with you,' or to say the same: 'God bless you! Keep warm and eat well!' –if you don't give them the necessities of life?"

And thirdly:

168

III. For Jesus Christ Peace is an Action which can be Commanded

Peace is not the excuse for the empires to keep the control of weaker countries. On the contrary, Jesus Christ as the "Prince of peace" (Is 9.5) is the one who seeks justice for all his creatures. Jesus will vindicate his suffering people.

Peace is not just an inner feeling of tranquility before God. Peace is not just a gift we have to be open to receive from God. For Jesus Christ, peace is a state of well being which enables us to help our neighbors to experience and live the same.

One of the beatitudes says: "Blessed are you the peace-makers because God will call you God's children." Jesus first forgave the sinful woman, and first healed the woman who was sick of hemorrhaging, and then he told them "Go in peace."

The risen Christ said "Irie!" or "Peace be with you" but at the same time he is showing us his perforated hands, like telling us that peace is something to be made real for our neighbors. That peace is not just a good feeling or a repression movement to keep things as they are. Peace is a state of experiencing the fullness of life and of doing something for everybody to live that: "As the Father sent me, so send I you."

Let me put it this way:

The old greeting "Peace be with you" or the modern greeting "Irie!" means the same: What can I do for you to experience and live God's shalom? What can I do for you to feel irie, for you to experience the fullness of life?

We have been sent by Jesus Christ to do something for everybody 169 to live a life of plenty: "As the Father sent me, so send I you."

One Crucian told me that people say *La Valley* is in the back of God's face, meaning that God doesn't care about that place. But he replied to people who believe this way: "o.k., my neighborhood is behind God's face, but when God spits, God always spits forward, not backwards!"

Irie!, peace, or Shalom be with you, means that no neighborhood is in the back of God's face. Shalom means that God doesn't spit upon anybody, that our mission is to share Jesus Christ's peace and that it involves the risk of having our hands also perforated for the people who just want to be alone with their souls and God. The peace-maker D. Hamilton Jackson, for instance, was the first editor to be arrested and thrown in jail for writing about injustices, or about peace without justice. The same happened to St. Thomian Rothschild Francis, "our Great Liberator" who opposed the rule of US Navy. Buddoe is but another example of what "Irie" means.

Regardless of the corporeal and external ways we greet each other, we, as Christians have the command of announcing the good news of a life of plenty in our saying: "Irie!" or in our Christian greeting "Peace be with you."

Peace means the fullness of life, and peace for my neighbor has to be attained neither through war, nor through just a nice feeling, but through our loving commitment in favor of our neighbor even if people perforate our hands.

170

39

JESUS' PROMOTION TO THE HALL OF FAME![60]

Mk. 16. 15-20

Tim Duncan, the Cruzan basketball star of San Antonio Spurs. Andrew Jones the baseball Atlanta' Braves favorite, from Aruba. Sami Sosa, the Dominican baseball Chicago Cubs hero of last season. Juan Igor Gonzalez the Puertorrican baseball player of the Texas Rangers. Valmy Thomas, the Puertorrican born of Crucians parents, and the first US major league baseball player. Claude A. Benjamin, the Crucian ranking composer who made it into the Songwriters Guild Hall of Fame in 1984. These names are some examples of what our modern world understands by ascension.

Last Thursday we Christians celebrated the Ascension Day of Jesus Christ but his ascension means something very different from the ascensions we just mentioned.

The Worldly Ascension means:

I. The Zero-sum Game

We have been told that ascension means being promoted to a higher position in a corporation, in politics, even within the Church. Ascension right now has to do with being successful with triumph in life, with the Zero-sum game where some people win, because other people lose.

We hear everywhere "everybody can make it," "just do it." Also the YMCA has the slogan: "we are the winning team" or the Nazi soldiers had in their belt buckle the saying "God is with us," but the fact is that some people ascended because other people descended and that is how the game is played where some people win because others lose.

Rockefeller's emporium so well known in the Virgin Islands started from scratch. In 1956 Laurence even donated half of St. John's island for a national park and now I can hear the saying "you see, everybody can make it" "everybody can be ascended into a benefactor." But the truth is that this world is playing the game where some win because others lose.

The plain fact is that the world, as it is organized today maintains very few ascended people and the vast majority are descending to death. Now, once in a while, the ruling class allows for one person here, another there, to be lifted into fame, power and glory. But this is a way of keeping alive the lie that "everybody can be promoted to the Hall of Fame."

Within Christianity things are very different.

The Divine Ascension means:

II. The Positive-sum Game

The ascension is one of the main articles of our faith. Sunday after Sunday we confess the Creed: "He ascended into heaven, and is seated at the right hand of the Father." However, by ascension we mean the positive-sum game where everybody wins.

Charles Darwin with the evolution theory preached the survival or ascension of the fittest. Now, Jesus Christ is preaching to us about our mission of ascending the weakest through God's message of love.

Jesus, the carpenter, the bricklayer, the artisan, the cook, the menial worker, has been taken up into heaven and has been also exalted by being seated at the right hand of the Father. But before and after his ascension, he continues through his disciples performing miracles, serving, loving, specially the most needy people. The mission

172

of the living Jesus Christ is to ascend every person who is down in the midst of disgrace, "the last will be the first."

Jesus has been risen into heaven but let us not forget that before that, "he descended into hell" and therefore, Jesus Christ knows by experience, that in order to play the game where everybody wins, he and his disciples have to continue fighting all evil powers that make people, countries, continents descend into hell.

500 years before Christ the maps of our planet were very false. 500 years ago maps were still very inaccurate. Right now, TV dictates how reality is, but we know that this description is like the maps of 500 years before Christ; it is very false. Today we hear that everything is fine, that we are progressing, that our economies are healthy, that we are ascending. However, reality tells us the opposite: There are neighborhoods, cities, countries, continents, descending more and more into under-life, into a subhuman situation which offends Jesus there, where he is sitting at the right hand of the Father.

In Short:
Jesus, the Carpenter from Nazareth, is still alive! Now, he, was ascended not into the Hall of Fame, nor the Guiness book of records, nor the Nobel prize, but into heaven. And in spite of such a heavenly promotion, his joy is not complete until everybody can join him in his place of honor.

Jesus, through his disciples, is still descending into hell, in order to ascend each and every one into heaven.

St. Iraneus said: "the glory of God is that people have life." Oscar Arnulfo Romero, the Salvadorean martyr and arschbishop corrected Iraneus: "The glory of God is that *poor* people have life." Jesus Christ suffers everytime we ascend things, pets or whatever and descend human beings.

173

Toussaint L'ouverture and others in 1804 ascended their country Haiti into heaven, by being the first independent country of the

Caribbean and Latin America. The United States took almost 60 years in order to accept their ascension. Unfortunately by now, Haiti needs a new ascension because other countries and people went back and descended the country into death.

Martiniquan Frantz Fanon, a psychiatrist world famous for his book *The Wretched of the Earth*, invested his life in lifting up to heaven his second country of Algeria, Africa. He could very well have played the game of winning because others would lose. He could have remained in France as a prestigious psychiatrist since he was very brilliant, but he preferred to play the game where everybody wins.

Eric Williams, the great economic historian from Trinidad and Tobago, did a terrific job as a scholar. He invested his life in ascending into heaven the descended people from his country, from the Caribbean, and from all over the world.

"He ascended into heaven, and is seated at the right hand of the Father" says our Creed, and we may add: "Jesus and his disciples continue descending into hell ad visiting every person who still remains way down in misery, in order to ascend them into a decent, free, dignified, and plentiful life."

174

40
LET'S GET TOGETHER AND FEEL ALRIGHT!
Acts 2.17-18

This morning we are celebrating the Feast of Pentecost, the feast of the Holy Spirit descending into each and every human being in order to unite us. That is precisely the meaning of the reggae hymn: "Let's get together and feel alright!"

The Feast of Pentecost was originally associated with the harvest (Exodus 23:16, 34:22) and eventually with the commandments given at Mount Sinai. But in the Book of Acts it takes on a new meaning. Luke digs deeply into the Hebrew Bible and quotes Joel 2: "In those days, I will pour out my Spirit over all humanity:

1. "your sons and daughters will proclaim my message, 2, your old people will dream dreams and your young people will see visions. 3. Even on my servants, in those days, I will pour out my Spirit."

First of all:

I. Pentecost Means Gender Justice 17.A

"Your sons and daughters will prophesy."

Paul, Luke's teacher, by divine inspiration would say the same: "In Jesus Christ there is no longer male or female." (Galatians 3:28)

In the church of Christ there can be no favoritism: machismo or feminism. In this unity there is no room for sayings such as: "for men any place I hang my hat is home."

We give thanks to God because the Crucian Lutheran Church,

among other branches of the Christian church has obeyed the example set by the Feast of Pentecost by ordaining women pastors, and surely enough, even women bishops. But we must not fool ourselves, we have not yet rid ourselves of certain prejudices and attitudes that the power of the Holy Spirit has to abolish. As yet we are unable to proclaim victory, instead we should stand together as a family against injustices that have prevailed to the detriment of the half of heaven, that is, women.

We should be on guard about "female machism" like in the story of the runaway slave Hagar, victim of domestic violence from Sara, Abraham's wife (Gn 16.6). Sara, the mother of the Israelites was an abusive woman.

Secondly:
II. Pentecost Means Generational Justice 17.B
"Your old people will dream dreams and your young people will see visions."

The consumer society that we live in preaches the contrary. This perverse world idolizes youth and their slim figure as though it were an ordinary piece of merchandise. Almost a century ago, Oscar Wilde would worship endless pleasure and eternal youth. In his novel *The Portrait of Dorian Grey* this mentality has robbed our youth of the vision of a society without wars, without hunger, without hate, and also has made us think of our elderly as a social burden, as useless. "Living la vida loca" is but another version of the same "Doriangreyism."[61]

176

The Feast of Pentecost celebrates the old people. The prophet Joel reminds us that thanks to the elderly we are not orphans of dreams. That today's society contrary to the Reign of God should not see itself as God wanted.

The Feast of Pentecost also celebrates youth. It celebrates the young visionaries that kept the flame of justice, of truth, of beauty, of goodness alive. The Christian youth is always visionary and with it works hand in hand with the older generation, to build a more humane society.

There are many spiritual songs regarding the elderly task of dreaming dreams: "Children, we shall be free/ when the Lord shall appear? Give ease to the sick, give sight to the blind/ enable the cripple to walk;/ He'll raise the dead from under the earth,/ and give them permission to talk." The elderly not only handed out history, they also dreamed dreams for better times: "When Israel was in Egypt's land,/ let my people go;/ Oppressed so hard they could not stand; / let my people go,/ Go down, Moses, 'way down in Egypt's land;/ Tell ole Pharaoh/ Let my people go."

Youth will see visions, like in the spiritual song: "My Lord delivered Daniel, My Lord delivered Daniel, My Lord delivered Daniel, Why can't He deliver me?/ Or maybe you prefer this one: "Freedom at last!/ Freedom at last!/ Great God-al-mighty,/ Freedom at last."

I will go on to my final reflection:

III. Pentecost Means Economic Justice 18.

"Even on my servants in those days, I will pour out my Spirit..." Or like Paul said it: "In Jesus Christ there is no longer slave or free."

In the Letter of Philemon written by the year 53 or 54, we find the story of his slave Onesimus who used to live in the city of Colossae. Slaves hardly reached the age of 35. They usually got their freedom around the age of 25 or 30 when they were useless for hard work. According to Mt 18.25 slaves were sold to solve debts. In Lk 17.7-9 we know that they never had a day off. We must confess once and for all, in light of the Feast of Pentecost that we are about 2000 years behind. The economic ties between rich countries and the poor countries, is getting worse. The new world order is actually an established disorder.

In the Feast of the Pentecost like in the judgment of the nations in

177

Matthew 25, the poor have a place of honor. And this is the core of the message of the the spiritual songs as well: Oh Lord, I'm hungry/ I want to be fed./ O Lord, I'm hungry/ I want to be fed,/ O feed me Jesus, feed me, / Feed me all my days./ O Lord, I'm naked/ I want to be clothed, / O Lord, I'm naked/ I want to be clothed,/ O clothe me Jesus clothe me,/ Clothe me all my days./

Or maybe your favorite is this protest Pentecost song: De fare is cheap, an' all can go,/ De rich an' poor are dere,/ No second class a -board did train,/ No difference in de fare./ Git on board, little chillen, Git on board, little chillen, Git on board little chillen, Dere's room for many a mo'.

In Brief:

The devil comes from two Latin words: *dia-bolos* which means to separate, to divide. The Feast of the Spirit, on the other hand means unity.

From Pentecost Feast follows gender, age, and economic justice. One astrounat said when he was on the moon: "The Earth fits in my hand; I can't see in her divisions of people, of beliefs. The Earth is our common home, our cosmic motherland. We have to learn to love this magnificent white and blue planet, because the Earth is being threatened." Our universe name comes from *universum*, "to go back to unity." Onion also means unity, since it comes from *unio*, plant of a single bulb.

On this Pentecost Sunday why don't we break the chain of oppression: "father abusing mother; mother mistreating children; children kicking the dog; the dog biting father."

Let's get together and feel alright!

178

41
THE AFRICAN MAN WHO SPONSORED JESUS CHRIST
Mark 15.21-28

First of all, let me congratulate you because of your birthday! the day of the Holy Cross, namely, Saint Croix's Day! Crucian's Day!

The origin of this feast is dated back in the 7th century but we can trace it as far back as the 4th century: In 326 Helen, the mother of the Roman emperor Constantine, did a pilgrimage to Jerusalem where she claimed to have found the *Veracruz*, that is the true cross of Jesus. People attributed healing powers to that cross and pieces of the same were sent throughout the empire.

In 614 the Byzantine emperor Heraclius (575-641) returned the *Veracruz* to Jerusalem, the true cross which was stolen by the Persians. Heraclius escorted the Cross in person into Jerusalem but he got stuck all of a sudden. Zachariah, the Archbishop of Jerusalem told him that his luxurious clothes and his golden crown didn't go with the humble Jesus of the cross. Heraclius got rid of his fine cape and shoes and then was able to escort the cross. Pieces of the cross were sent to Rome, to Constantinople, and to the entire world in order to preach and witness the humble Jesus Christ!

Today's gospel tells us about Simon of Cyrene, Africa, who carried Jesus' cross. Allow me to share some thoughts about Simon of Cyrene carrying Jesus' cross.

First:

I. Simon of Cyrene

Egypt, Ethiopia and other places from Africa are very important in the Bible. Here we are before another African region very relevant for the biblical message: Cyrene.

Bible teachers and prophets like African Lucius reached the famous Christian community of Antioch (Acts 13.1). On Pentecost day the Holy Spirit descended also upon the people from Cyrene (Acts 2.10). Some persons from Cyrene became members of the synagogue of Jerusalem (Acts 6.9). Alexander and Rufus, the two children of Simon of Cyrene, were two well respected and well known Africans, most probably members of the Christian community of Rome (Rom 16.13).

Cyrene was part of Libya in Mediterranean Northern Africa. Precisely from this African city, this morning we are reminded about Simon, the passing-by fellow who helped Jesus to carry the cross!

Simon from Cyrene did such a good job in bearing Jesus' cross that rumor and gossip was spread in the sense that Simon the African substituted Jesus on the Cross. People still think that it was Simon of Cyrene the one who was crucified in order to save Jesus' life!

Now, let's consider the rest of our story: Simon of Cyrene carrying Jesus' cross:

II. Jesus' Cross

Cross is one of the most deceiving words.

A) For North Atlantic countries the cross and the sword are still like hand and glove! Christopher Columbus re-baptized the Island of Ay-Ay with the name Santa Cruz, and in every new place Columbus stepped, he planted a cross as a sign of taking possession, as a sign of stealing that land! The crosses of the flags from England, Knights of Malta and Denmark, also have that imperialistic motivation!

For centuries the Christian movement called the Crusades, linked the cross with killing people, killing cultures, expropriating lands.

For hundreds of years the not so Holy Inquisition assassinated so many people, out of which 85% were women, all in the name of the cross. This unhappy institution disappeared people who fought for a more humane society.

Klansmen wearing white cloaks and hoods in the Ku Klux Klan, despite their protestant roots, are known as cross burners as they kill and destroy the properties of Afro-Americans and Immigrants among other communities.

Now,

B) For Southern countries the cross means liberation.

In 1638, during the 2nd siege of Vienna by the Turks, bakers heard in the middle of the night how the Turks were excavating a tunnel. The bakers made everybody alert and Vienna frustrated the surprise attack. As a reward to the bakers, they were allowed to create a new type of bread: an Arab half moon, in order to remember that the holy Cross defeated the Arab half moon, the name of that bread was croix sainte or cross saint, better known as *Croissant*.

For the African slaves the cross of Christ meant God's solidarity with them even to the extreme of God offering His life. Jesus was with them and, they were with Jesus: "Where you there when they crucified my Lord" they asked, and they themselves answered, "we, together with Simon of Cyrene, we were there accompanying God as Jesus Christ was accompanying us until the end, bringing us life, bringing us freedom!"

181

We Lutherans only inherited from Luther the making of the sign of the cross. But we Hispanics have 2 verbs and 2 gestures related with the cross. Santiguarse (to make the sign of the cross) "means to sanctify or consecrate: it takes the form of a sign of the cross and a Trinitarian invocation. 'Persignarse' (to sign oneself) is a cumulative and repetitive action, as in persuading, pursuing, or perturbing, and refers more appropriately to the triple cross on the forehead, on the lips and on the chest. The words which are spoken are a request for protection: "'Through the sign of the holy cross, free us from our enemies, Lord'. Here the motive is one of protection, in contrast to the sign of the cross which has the purpose of consecration."[62]

In synthesis:

The cross is central to our Christian faith: *Crux sola est nostra theologia* said Martin Luther, that is, "the cross alone is our theology," but the cross as a symbol of life and not of death.

Jesus of Nazareth could very well have died at home, surrounded by his dear ones, at an advanced age. But Jesus chose to give himself to the suffering people even to give his life on the cross. The cross is the constant reminder of God's self-giving, of God's for-giving, of God's emptying Himself in favor of all humanity.

Simon of Cyrene, the man who sponsored Jesus, points towards God's self-giving but also God's receiving, God's accepting the help of this African fellow.

Baby Jesus found solidarity in Egypt, Africa, from the persecution of King Herod the Great. Mature Jesus found solidarity in the African Simon of Cyrene, from the persecution of the Roman Empire.

The crucified God rejects the image of a self-sufficient, almighty and all powerful God, who doesn't need anything from anybody. The crucified God introduces himself as a dependent God, a needy God, a vulnerable God. In short, Simon of Cyrene's presence in the Gospel tells us that God needs us! That God moves his plans forward with our help! That Jesus wouldn't have accomplished his extreme self-giving and for-giving on the cross for the entire humanity without the help of the African Simon of Cyrene!

Were you there when they crucified my Lord? Yes, Crucians were there! Happy birthday Saint Croix, the symbol of life, of freedom, of solidarity!

182

42
CAN'T YOU PREACH?
Luke 5.1-11

It is a bad line to credit Europeans and Euro-Americans for the protestant evangelization of the Caribbean. Nevertheless, the truth is quite different. European planters brought their Christian denominations with them to the West Indies: Danes and Lutheranism; Dutch and the Reformed faith; British and the Episcopal tradition; Spaniards and Roman Catholicism. Roman Catholicism came with Christopher Columbus in 1493. By the way, Columbus re-baptized these lands as the Virgin Islands after the legendary Christian martyrs Ursula and her 11,000 fellow virgins who were murdered by the Huns at Cologne while returning from pilgrimage to Rome, the 21st of October, in the 3rd century.

The Moravian faith was for the slaves, but, and this is an important but, Moravians didn't take the initiative. Anthony Ulrich,[63] an Afro-Saint Thomian slave deserves the honor. In 1731 this slave was taken to Copenhagen with his master Count Ferdinand Danneskjold Laurvig, who didn't want to miss Christian VI's coronation. In Denmark, Anthon or Anthony met the founder of the Moravians, Count Nicholas Zinzendorf, and shared with him the sorry conditions of the West Indies slaves. Anthony even went to Saxoney with Zinzendorf in order to get things ready for doing missionary work in the Caribbean.

The slaves worked from can't to can't: "I can't see in the morning to I can't see in the night," that is, from 5.00 a.m to 6.30 pm.

Therefore, the Moravian missionaries who arrived by 1732, had to take time after 6.30 pm in order to share their Christian faith with the slaves.

Whether Moravian missionaries knew it or not, they were doing exactly what Jesus did: to share the good news of the Gospel to busy people who were right there, at their place of work. The first disciples of Jesus Christ were two sets of brothers who were in the midst of washing their nets having them ready for the next fishing trip. They just left everything and followed Jesus when he asked them: can't you preach?

The liberating gospel of Jesus Christ hasn't spread out all over the world due to the eloquent preaching of pastors, or due to the well delivered speech of famous evangelists. No. The gospel of Jesus Christ is all over the world thanks to the working people like the first fishermen, and thanks to the people like the sugar workers of the West Indies who, in the midst of their tiring journey decided to follow Jesus immediately.

This Mission Sunday we need to keep in mind that, from the very beginning, the gospel of Jesus Christ meant to the Afro-american people to follow Jesus immediately, in spite of their exhausting work schedule. For Afro-American folks church was not a leisure time activity, on the contrary, it was a discipleship which took place in the midst of dozens of other responsibilities. But they just left everything and followed Jesus as he asked them: can't you preach?

Let me illustrate this point with a little bit of history.

Historians usually affirm that the Protestant faith arrived in Puerto Rico due to the missionary work of the Swedish Gustav Sigfrid Swensson. They also state that it was a baptist pastor and army chaplain who celebrated the first worship in Puerto Rico. But we are missing something very important. Browne, an Afro-Jamaican man came to the Virgin Islands and converted to Lutheranism, later he made his home in Puerto Rico. And look what happened. But let us hear the Swedish Swensson relate his story personally:

"It happened that on the 3rd of December, 1898, when I was walking home from one of my classes that coming up Sol street an English Afro-Jamaican was standing in the doorway at #87 and as he beheld my insignificant being passing by said to me: "how do you do! You look like a man of God. Can't you preach?" I stopped and returned greetings and although the Afro-Jamaican, with whom I was not acquainted, did not look very dignified, yet I advanced toward him and with a blush on my face such as I never felt before... After I conversed with Mr. Browne, for that was the Afro-Jamaican name, I promised him to come again on the morrow, Sunday, and conduct a meeting at 9.30 am. Sunday, the 4th of December, 1898, came and the first Protestant meeting was held in San Juan. In the morning about eight attended and in the evening about thirty."[64]

Now, what Swensson didn't mention is that mainly Virgin Islanders who worshiped God that morning were busy people. Browne was a tailor. George did body work on cars. Beverhardt, a St. Thomian was a typographer, many women were domestic employees, and the majority of those 38 first followers of Jesus were from the Virgin Islands and were working busy folks! But they just left everything and followed Jesus as he asked them: can't you preach?

All of this means that the protestant faith didn't arrive in Puerto Rico due to the Swedish efforts but to the Afro-Caribbean missionaries. All of this also means that, exactly like in our gospel story of this morning, the first followers of Jesus Christ in Puerto Rico were menial workers, busy people, who were reached by Jesus precisely in their work environment.

The gospel for this morning reminds us that Christianity is not for idle people who don't know how to kill time. Christianity is not a leisure time activity or a show time as if it were one more of the amusement industries of entertainment.

185

Christianity is for working and busy people like the fishermen of our story. Christianity is for hardworking folks like our ancestors who, after a long and inhumane journey of working, were eager to listen to the Word of God and followed him. Christianity is for brothers and sisters like the Virgin Islanders in Puerto Rico who were the first missionaries.

The story of this morning tells us about Jesus' first calling to discipleship. And it tells us about the two sets of brothers who, in spite of being very busy, left everything and said yes to Jesus' question: can't you preach? The same happened in the Virgin Island plantations, the workers just said yes to Jesus precisely because Jesus prefers the busy people to the idle people. The same took place in Denmark with St. Thomian Anthony Ulrich who was providential in bringing the Moravian faith to the Virgin Islands. The same took place in Puerto Rico, when Browne the tailor, the artisans, the teachers, the peasants, without blaming it on their busy schedules, said yes to the invitation of following Jesus and now we can say that the Lutheran Church of the Virgin Islands is the mother of the Lutheran church of Puerto Rico.

It would be great if some Crucian women and men would go to the seminary in order to be ordained deaconesses or pastors. But, Jesus' calling this morning is for everybody who is ready to follow him in the midst of our busyness, in the midst of out working environments. Brothers and sisters, the liberating gospel of Jesus Christ has reached all the continents not because of the work of the theologians, pastors or evangelists, but because of the work of the busy, working people who have said yes to Jesus' question: Can't you preach?

186

43
SILENCING THE PAST[65]
John 8.31-36

Virgin Islanders have never conquered other countries, have never taken away their names, their languages, their history, but unfortunately we live in a forgetful world.

"Don't read history, make history" is the propaganda the army uses to recrute people. "Don't read history, make history" is also the short-term that the media broadcasts. "Don't read history, make history is a call to forget about the past and to lie about the present. This short-term vision is precisely the theme that this Reformation Sunday is against.

Silencing the past, inventing the present and not contemplating the future is what these colonized people are doing in the Biblical text we just read. This is so because:

I. Colonized Folks Silenced the Past

Jesus just told his audience: "the truth will set you free" but the colonized persons prefer lies than truth. The word *truth* comes from two Greek words: *a* -no and *lethe* -forgetfulness. Truth is *aletheia,* or no-forgetfulness. In order for us to reach freedom we have to start by remembering our history, who we are.

The truth will set you free said Jesus and the colonized angrily answered: "we have never been anybody's slaves." Those Jews were liars because truth means: not to forget and they already forgot their country had been under more than seven empire flags: the

Egyptian, the Babylonian, the Philistine, the Amorite, the Assyrian, the Syrian, the Persian, the Greek, etc. and at that very moment they were a colony of the Roman empire! How absent minded could they be? For sure they didn't read history, they pretended to make history."

These colonized leaders not only forgot about their political dominations, they also condemned the memory (*damnatio memoriae*) of the widows, the orphans, the foreigners, but Jesus told them: if you want to be free, you should not silence the past. Contrary to the colonized people's forgetfulness, we have the fact that:

II. Caribbeans Folks Do Remember

Rubén Blades, the song composer and singer hasn't silenced the past. He has insisted for more than 30 years on the importance of knowing our history. He was born in Panama, he inherited his musical talents from St. Lucia, on his father's side; his singing skills are a gift from Cuba through his mother's genealogy. The Blades arrived from St. Lucia to build the Panama Canal under the supervision of the US Army. Virgin Islanders remember that instead of ameliorating the living conditions many of them also died in that Canal due to malaria and exhausting work. Rubén Blades' chronicle-songs command us "if you believe in your flag and if you believe in freedom then, "forgetting is prohibited".

Alejo Carpentier, the Cuban journalist and novelist didn't silence the past. In his historical novel *The Kingdom of this World* (1949), he remembered the fight of the French main colony, Haiti, until it conquered freedom. Carpentier knew that we shouldn't "silence the past", so he remembered the central role the creole language, sacred drums, story telling, voodoo religion, played in their struggle for freedom.

Frantz Fanon, the Martiniquan psychiatrist, writer and social

188

activist, didn't silence the past. In 1943 he stood in solidarity with the struggle for freedom of the sister Island of Dominique. In 1944 he opposed Nazism. Since 1953 he made his own the cause of Algeria, where more than a million Africans were killed in a period of eight years. In his book *The Wretched of the Earth* (1961), Fanon tells us not to forget that like a boomerang, violence exercised by the European army against Africa, America and Asia is followed by a counter-violence in response. Death didn't allow him to go to Cuba, but his heroic memory is more intense day by day in the Caribbean.

Andrés Eloy Blanco, the Venezuelan poet didn't silence the past. Andrés Eloy showed us that "silencing the past" has to do not only with the history of the Earth, but also with the history of Heaven. He dared to reject heavenly racism in his immortal poem: *Paint me little black angels*. Little angels doesn't mean to diminish the heavenly beings, it is only the tender diminutive typical of the Afro-Indian cultures' way of talking: "You, painter who paints with love/ why do you despise my color?/ If you know that in heaven/ African-Americans are very dear to God as well!

Don't silence the past was also known in the 16th century because:

III. Reformers Do Remember

The Christian churches have been engaged with the truth, or the need of not silencing the past. Until the Middle Ages Christians honored the old members because they were the custodians of the past. John Calvin is the spiritual father of Presbyterians who took their name from *Presbyter*, which means elder person. Senator also means elder person. Old people were considered in high esteem because they didn't silence the past, on the contrary, they handed it down to the newer generations.

The teaching and worshiping of the Christian church is a constant reminder for us not to silence the past. For instance, today we

189

remember Reformation Sunday and how Martin Luther set the church free from so many human burdens. Luther set his Germany free from foreign Roman oppressors. Luther set his German language free from the imperialistic Latin. Zwingli and Luther set pastors free from being forced to remain single. Luther set the poor people free from paying a lot of money for religious services. But, unfortunately, Luther didn't say a word in relation to slave trade and the planting of European flags on this continent!

To put it more simply:

The first step to reach freedom is to know the truth, and truth means not to forget. Truth means not silencing your past.

Crucians don't take the army invitation seriously: "Don't read history, make history." What Crucians do instead is to remember that you have been under seven flags and that, in spite of that, your remember your roots, your own heroes, our own way of doing things.

Christians don't take the army invitation seriously: "Don't read history, make history." Instead of that, we read, we listen, and we rember our history as it is magnificently demonstrated in Jesus' eating habits: "Do this in remembrance of me."

Caribbean slavery started in 1503 and ended in 1886. It lasted almost four centuries, and all of the colonial powers planted their flag in St. Croix. But the liberating news is Virgin Islanders have never conquered other countries, have never taken away their names, their languages, their cuisines, their history. The liberating news is that Jesus doesn't silence the past, because He not only addressed the issue of truth, but He himself is the truth. Therefore, on this Reformation Sunday, sisters and brothers, don't silence the past.

44
ST. MARTIN OF TOURS
Mt 25.31-46

The day before yesterday Buenos Aires, Argentina celebrated the day of its protector, Saint Martin of Tours (c.335-c.400). He was a Hungarian Order founder and bishop of the 4th century. He was predestined by his very name to be a warrior: Martin —Mars— "warrior God." At the age of 15 he became a soldier of the Roman empire.

All of us are familiar with two words of his legacy: Chapel and chaplain. But let us listen to the old and new versions of St. Martin of Tours history:

I. The Old Version

The 10-year old boy Martin became Christian against his parents will. After 5 years his father wanted for his son to break with his Christian fellows, so his father sent Martin into the army. One day, Martin, the soldier, was getting into the Italian city of Amiens when one beggar who was freezing because of the cold snow asked him for some money. Martin didn't have money to give him, but he immediately tore up his cloak in two and divided one half to the beggar to survive the cold winter. That night, Martin dreampt about Jesus Christ who was wearing Martin's half cloak telling him: "whenever you did this for one of the least important brothers and sisters of mine, you did it for me!"

Martin's sharing of his half cloak with the beggar became so well known that, from that good deed became our words of chapel and chaplain which means half a cloak. The church where the half cloak was kept as a relic became known as the chapel, and the cloak custodian became known as the chaplain. In this case, in Spanish it is clearer: cloak is capa, chapel is capilla, and chaplain is capellán. Capa, capilla, capellán means cloak, chapel, chaplain.

After the vision, Martin was baptized, left the army and became a monk and later bishop. The feast of Saint Martin of Tours of November 11, has been a very popular celebration in Germany since the Middle Ages. Children hold torches, sing, and have processions to different chapels.

II. The Modern Version[66]

Lately things are changing, by the end of our 20th century there is a new version of the history of Saint Martin of Tours.

A young good looking and well established man is walking on the street on a cold winter night when he sees a beggar lying on the snow asking for money. This young man whose name is Ludwig, like the German Ministry of Economy Ludwig Erhard, doesn't believe in sharing. In fact, Ludwig hates Saint Martin of Tours feast and has proposed to eliminate it. When the beggar talked to Ludwig asking him for money, Ludwig didn't care, and about the possibility of sharing his coat with the beggar, forget it. What Ludwig did say to the beggar was: "No! I won't give you any money, because that is much better for you" and Ludwig turned his back on the beggar right away.

According to this modern version of Saint Martin of Tours, the beggar was so shocked with Ludwig's answer. The beggar stopped asking for money in the streets, instead of that, the beggar opened a small business and from then on, he made his living out of his own efforts. The beggar was of the idea that if Ludwig had shared his money or his coat with him he would've continued to be spoiled. During his whole life the beggar was so thankful to Ludwig for not sharing his money with him.

"Kingshill Lutheran Church" is honored to host this morning chapter *Mu Gamma Omega* of the *Alpha Kappa Alpha* Sorority. And we are doubly honored by realizing that Professor Winona A. Hendriks, a liturgist of our church is also the president of *Mu Gamma Omega* chapter. We want to congratulate you for the 22nd anniversary you are celebrating this weekend. *Alpha Kappa Alpha* is the oldest sorority established in America by Afro American Women, with over 200,000 women in Bermuda, Bahamas, England, Germany, Korea and Japan among other countries.

Sor is the contraction of the Latin word *Sóror* which means "sister." Sorority then, is another way of saying sisterhood.

Sororities, these voluntary, nonprofit organizations were formed to promote sisterhood and brotherhood or, friendship relationships. These Greek letter societies started working exclusively with women in 1851, precisely in a Methodist college, at Macon Ga., always inculcating the values of promoting friendship relationships and charity.

Dear sisters of *Mu Gamma Omega* chapter of the *Alpha Kappa Alpha* sorority, or sisterhood, you may hide your rituals, you may have a secret handclasp, you may not share your motto or a badge of external display. But, for sure you can't hide your high ideals of the promotion of friendship relationships through good deeds.

We thank God for your generous donations of books to the Queen Louise Home. For the educational scholarships you provide. For the materials and supplies you give to the Governor Juan Luis Hospital. For supporting Flamboyant Senior Citizens Home, and for many more fruits you are bearing as the gospel for this morning encourages us to do.

193

Sisterhood, brotherhood or to give is the mark of the Christian church. Let us hold hands with all the sororities and fraternities in order to oppose grabbing and to promote giving. Let us learn together how to be givers and not receivers. In order to be rich in good deeds. Thank you dear sisterhood, thank you dear sorority for reminding us today what it means to consecrate our lives to serve our neighbors.

Let me piggyback to our story.

Buenos Aires's protector, Saint Martin of Tours is a constant reminder of giving like he gave one half of his cloak. Ludwig from Germany, on the contrary, says: "No! I won't give you anything, because that is much better for you." To give or not to give, that is the question. The order of the *Opus Dei* openly promotes the apostolate of not giving; *Mu Gamma Omega* Sorority openly promotes the apostolate of giving.

May Jesus Christ's words of the Last Judgement (Mt 25.34) apply not only to St. Martin of Tours, not only to our Sorority we honor today, but to all of us: "Come you that are blessed by my Father! Come and possess the kingdom which has been prepared for you ever since the creation of the world."

May we continue practicing the words of the Afro-American song:

O Lord, I'm hungry
I want to be fed.
O Lord, I'm hungry
I want to be fed,
O feed me Jesus, feed me,
Feed me all my days.
O Lord, I'm naked
I want to be clothed,
O Lord, I'm naked
I want to be clothed,
O clothe me Jesus, clothe me,
Clothe me all my days.

194

45
GET UP AND WALK
Mark 2. 1-12

"Get up and walk" reminds us of the Aztec Indian greeting: "don't allow yourself to fall, because if you fall you will fall forever."

"Get up and walk" tells us that our God is a God that walks the whole time, a God that doesn't allow Godself to fall. We find God walking in the garden of Eden with Adam and Eve. We find Jesus constantly on the move especially in this gospel of Mark. He walks in procession to Jerusalem, he walks up the mountains, and down the valleys. In fact there is only one time that the gospel reports that he rode a donkey. Maybe he also rode a camel or a horse, but for sure he was an untiring walker. One of the first names to call Christians was "the people of the road," that is, people on the move, or walking people.

"Get up and walk" is related with a 19th century Danish Lutheran pastor, Søren Kierkegaard. He got involved in pastoral counseling to his sister-in-law Henriette Kierkegaard (Jette), who spent a great deal of time in bed with harsh mental depressions. Soon after one visit to Jette, Søren continued encouraging his sister-in-law to go out and walk, as he himself used to do for an hour and a half sometimes:[67]

Above all, do not lose your desire to walk: every day I walk myself into a state of well-being and walk away from every illness; I have walked myself into my best thoughts, and I know of no thought so burdensome that one cannot walk away from it. Even if one were to walk for one's health and it were constantly one station ahead-I would still say: Walk! Besides, it is also apparent that in walking one constantly gets as close to well-being as possible, even if one does not quite reach it. But by sitting still, and the more one sits still, the closer one comes to feeling ill. Health and salvation can be found only in motion. If anyone denies that motion exists, I do as Diogenes did, I walk. If anyone denies that health resides in motion, then I walk away from all morbid objections. Thus, if one just keeps on walking, everything will be all right. [68]

This Lutheran pastor urged Jette to be "actively engaged in life," to not consider worrying a necessity, to go beyond her small rooms and have frequent airing out, to inhale "good and beneficial and gentle and soothing thoughts." [69]

"Get up and walk" has to do with the style of life of Jesse Owens. He was, in many ways, the greatest Afro-American athlete of the 20th century. In the Olympic Games in Berlin 1936, Hitler's plans were to use the games to demonstrate Aryan superiority. Jesse Owens won 4 gold medals and spoiled Hitler's feast. Despite all the honor he won for USA, he lived in poverty and he was forgotten. But, every time Jesse was facing some problem he had a magic formula. He used to say: "Why don't we work things out while we walk."

"Get up and walk" is the invitation Jesus made to all of us in Capernaum, a crossroads town. We find Jesus performing the miracle of sending a paralyzed man back to the road. Because to walk means to be alive, because to be on the move means *not to lose your desire to walk*, it means: to greet each other: "don't allow yourself to fall, because if you fall you will fall forever." It means to use Jesse Owen's magic formula: "Why don't we work things out while we walk."

It is not for nothing that one of our most unconscious actions is walking. Each culture in fact has its own way of walking: with short

196

and jumping steps, or with long and balancing steps, or in hundreds of different ways. Today some psychologists are able to study our character by means of analyzing the wearing down of our shoes.

"Get up and walk" is Jesus' commandment, because to walk means to be alive, to not allow ourselves to fall, not to allow ourselves to lose the desire to walk. "To work things out while we walk."

The 20th century is a century of cars. You heard in the news this week how 30 something cars crashed into each other in California. In 1984 the estimate of people been killed in car accidents was of 50,000 per year only in USA. I don't have the figures of last year but just think of the superabundance of cars and the suicidal way of driving while using cellular phones and other distractors.

"Get up and walk" is Jesus' commandment and he added: "take your mat" which means get rid of your mat. What are our modern mats that don't allow us to walk and be healed? Besides cars, the TV which bewitches us and keeps us attached to it wasting our time and losing our desire to walk. The refrigerator is also an obstacle for some people to walk. The comfortable sofa, the nice bed, who knows what are our modern mats that keep us from keeping on walking to the next stage.

"Get up and walk" also means to be free. It is not an accident that walking has been a weapon for seeking justice. Martin Luther King's famous marches united walking with the struggle for civil rights. It is not for nothing that people who fought for freedom where called "run-aways." And the runaways literally walked and walked until the end of the roads in order to achieve their freedom. Tomorrow thousands of Christians will be marching as a way of struggling for peace in Vieques. In the decade of the 1940's there was an attempt to bring to St. Croix all the Puertorricans that were living in Vieques in order to use the whole island for bombarding. After more than 60 years we still find people walking as a way of protesting against that action.

197

"Get up and walk" means continue walking until the following station, and do it with your head up. For centuries many of our ancestors had their neck paralyzed. They were not allowed to raise their heads while walking in front of the powerful people. For centuries our ancestors where not allowed to walk on the sidewalks, these were reserved for the people who wore shoes and fancy clothes. But we not only hear Jesus telling everybody "Get up and walk," raise your head. God goes further and tells us in the book of Revelation 21.21 that in the New Jerusalem "The streets will be of pure gold." That doesn't mean that the streets we hope to walk on are very important, what it means is that gold is not going to be important at all in the New City of Jerusalem. Gold is going to be something that we can step on. Gold is not to separate people into those who can walk on fancy streets and those who cannot. Gold is not going to separate people into those who can walk into some exclusive places and people who cannot. The warnings like "no trespassing" or "private property" are not part of the Kingdom of God because there we can walk without any walls that refrain us from continuing to walk.

Brothers and sisters, let us "Get up and walk." Like the Aztec greeting says, do not allow yourself to fall, because if you fall, you will fall forever." Let us bear in mind the wise piece of advice of that Lutheran pastor: *Above all, do not lose your desire to walk.*" Let us take with us the wise formula of Jesse Owens: "Why don't we work things out while we walk?" Let us follow the Afro American hymn invitation:

198

> I got shoes, you got shoes,
> All God's children got shoes.
> When I get to heb'n gonna put on my shoes,
> Gonna walk all over God's heb'n.
> Everybody talk'n 'bout heb'n
> ain't going there. Heb'n.

46
THE INCOMPLETE FLOCK
Luke 15. 1-7

Robert L. Lewis the copilot of Enola Gay, after dropping the atomic bomb on Hiroshima in 1945 stated: "Oh my God... what have we done?"

A pilot going back to the United States after the first air raid on Baghdad during the Gulf war commented regarding the bombarding and explosions during the night: "it looked just like a beautiful Christmas tree!"[70]

Maybe some day, through the black boxes, we will hear the last words of the suicidal pilots of the four commercial airplanes, that terrorized strategic places in the United States last Tuesday, September the 11th.

Sisters and brothers, the parable for this morning is an invitation to reflect about why there is so much hate, so much revenge, so much arrogance in our world today. Let me begin by acknowledging that the real name of the parable we just read is "the incomplete flock" and not "the lost sheep" as we have traditionally called it. "The lost sheep" points towards rampant individualism; "The incomplete flock" encourages us to live in a loving community.

The other day I was talking a little bit with the Trini-Crucian Monty Thompson. He was telling me that one time when he was in Africa he went to the open supermarket where, as usual, the merchants of the same products stay in the same section. He heard the criticism of people from another culture: "why don't these merchants spread out? They should offer their products in distant spots from one another." The Crucian fellow explained to them that first of all, African culture does not value an individualistic and competitive society where everybody has to take distance from one another. Secondly, he told the tourist, when Africans sell their products they don't limit themselves just to establish a monosyllabic conversation: "How much does it cost? - Three dollars - I'll take it - O.K., bye." No, no. When the people from that African village sell their products they establish a warm relationship with their customers. They establish a trusting relationship in such a way that, even if there are a dozen spots around selling the same product, the customer has already established a loyalty with a merchant and the other merchants will respect that relationship. In Mexico the merchant and the custumer call each other "marchanta/marchante", from the word "merchant."

The parable of the "incomplete flock" was used by Jesus in order to criticize the individualism of his time. Jesus was extremely generous. Even if 99% of society are doing well, he will still insist on saving the 1% of the lost-now-found and then he will lift them up on his shoulders (Is 40.11). In our 21rst century the world percentage consists of 35% of privileged people and 65% of lost people because of unemployment and hunger.

The Mathematics of our time are very different. Rockefeller, at some time one of the biggest property owners of the Virgin Islands, used to say: In order to reach the beautiful red roses called "American beauty," you have to prune the ugly ones. Which in reality means, in order to have beautiful people you have to prune the ugly. But the liberating news of Jesus Christ is that not a single human being should be pruned!

200

Dear brothers and sisters, we are sad and hurt because of the terrorist actions that took place in New York, Washington and Pittsburgh. Lutherans, the Pope, and in general the protestant community already repudiated this kind of violence. There's no doubt. Christians oppose terror, violence, hate.

Nevertheless, instead of declaring war, it must be a time of meditation. Instead of asking who could be the terrorist? And how many were they, 20, 50, hundreds? It is a time to ask the right question: "why did this tragedy take place? Why do we live in an individualistic and divided world?

The African Anglican bishop Desmond Tutu said: "if everybody would follow the rule of thumb: of an eye for an eye and a tooth for a tooth, all of us would be without eyes and without teeth."

Let us not be confused, President Bush's declaration of the 21^{rst} century first war runs the risk of being a war against immigrants.

There are more than 600 white supremacist terrorist groups in the United States, like the one of the explosion in Oklahoma City. Nevertheless, President Bush from the very outset identified the Saudi Osama Bin Laden as the perpetrator of the terrorist action. President Bush doesn't consider this tragedy as a terrorist act against the few USA citizens who set the economic and military policy for the world. No. Bush considers this horrible event as a crime against humanity. However, let us keep in mind that USA is not the world. For example, why does USA call its national baseball season "The World Series"?, why is the USA a description of the whole continent? Anyhow, all humanity is hurt because of what happened in New York, Washington and the "accident of the fourth plane," because without them we will have an incomplete flock.

Jorge Batlle, the Uruguayan president, is of the opinion that what happened last Tuesday is not an act of war, it is an act of terrorism, and terrorism should be faced with a strong pacifist movement, a movement which has to include the Arab community. Jesus tells us this morning, if the Arabs are not present we will have an incomplete flock. This is not because there are 1.3 billion Arabs in the world; even if there was only one, the flock would be incomplete without she or he! We should love the many Arabs who have chosen US Virgin Islands as their second country.

201

Let us not be confused, President Bush's declaration of the 21ʳˢᵗ century first war runs the risk of being a war against the poor. Towers, beginning with the Tower of Babel, are a symbol of power and arrogance. The World Trade Center towers were a symbol of the current world economy which favors the very few and excludes billions of people. For instance, according to New York Major Rudolph Giuliani, by September 13th, it was 12 the number of Mexicans who died. Of course he counted only the very rare white collar or blue collar workers, but what about the hundreds of illegal Mexican, Haitian, Central American, and Asian workers who did the dirty jobs? In Jesus' Math, if you don't count them the flock is incomplete!

For a couple of days one third of the world's airplanes didn't fly. Only two United States airlines have more airplanes than Africa, The Caribbean and Latin America together! One sheep has the monopoly of the skies.

Let us not be confused President Bush's declaration of 21ʳˢᵗ century first war runs the risk of being a war against peace.

The "American Century," as United States baptized the 20ᵗʰ century, was a sign of war in: Te Dominican Republic, Cuba, Panama, Grenada, El Salvador, Nicaragua, to mention a few names, for you to know what we're talking about. Iraq has been bombarded for a decade, including these days, by British and American planes. Bombarding in Palestine is their everyday bread.

"Fortress America", the warrior America is symbolized by the Pentagon. "Five-sided forts are militarily ancient; five-pointed stars have supposedly magical properties in certain semotic systems,"[71] by certain pentacula, and seals and characters to fence themselves and to make themselves invisible against all kinds of arms and musquet bullets. In spite of that, the Pentagon was partially destroyed and now the answer is war and war means the annihilation f the other.

202

Let us be sure:

Unless some people and countries learn to love the immigrants, to take care of the poor and to be peacemakers we will never have a complete flock.

According to Noam Chomski, Colombia, Israel and Egypt, in that order, are the main customers of USA weapons.

Jesus' parable, on the contrary, warns us that it is only through peace, through diplomacy, that we will have a complete flock. War subtracts, war divides, war disbands the flock.

May our Liberator Jesus Christ assist us in building a kingdom for all races, where there is bread for everybody and a peaceful world neighborhood!

203

47

"COCOBEY ON TOP OF YAWS": THE WOMAN WHO DEFEATED CORRUPTION
Luke 18.1-8

What we know as the "parable of the persistent widow" is above all the "parable of a widow who fights for her rights".

This parable has to do with a bold woman who is emerging from her culture of silence to lifting up her voice. From her tradition of not doing anything against injustice to a new attitude of speaking out.

This is a story of a judge and a widow:

I. The Judge

was a cynical person. He openly confessed what used to be covertly accepted: he practiced bribery and corruption. He openly promoted injustice for, as the gospel says: "he neither feared God, nor had respect for people."

II. The Widow

in Jesus' time was supposed to be protected by God's law, according to Ex.22.22-24 and Deut 24.17. The Early Christian church destined the offering for burial expenses, for children lacking economic means, for taking care of the elderly, for supporting the destitute, and of course, for assisting widows economically, so that they didn't need to remarry.

However, this morning we are facing a widow who is requesting a judge: "grant me justice." What she is asking, most probably, is her maintenance from her husband's estate. Without her husband's money of the inheritance she had to remarry immediately in order to avoid starvation.

III. The Judge

knew his business and realized that women possessed rights in the Bible but not in real life. The judge knew that women were not allowed to put a foot on the court: women always had to be represented by a man and most probably this widow not even had a man close enough to stand up for her. This judge knew that widows were the easiest to dismiss. It is not for nothing that widows generally speaking were poor and destitute.

IV. The Widow

of our parable is a widow who is aware of her sorry situation. Still more, she is acquainted with her culture of remaining in silence. She learned from her childhood not to fight the unjust system, that is, not to call things by their own name, or not to tell the truth, in this case, about issues related with justice.

V. The Judge

needless to say, is in control. Women and especially widows were defenseless. The legal system, the religious system, the military system, the ruling system, all of them agreed that widows were practically without rights.

VI. The Widow

however, is full of surprises. She is not the kind of submissive woman who always repeats to herself: "nothing will change things." Not at all! This widow, instead shows herself as a bold person. An assertive woman who begins by breaking the mold of "nothing will change reality." She sure found her way of changing things: If the judge wasn't granting her justice, the widow in exchange didn't

205

respect the judge's office hours and the Bible tells us that she "kept on vexing him" like a Caribbean mosquito.

"Cocobey on top of yaws" ("leprosy on top of sores", that is, to make things worse), if the judge wasn't granting her justice, the widow in exchange didn't respect the judge's privacy and began making public this act of injustice!

VII. The Judge
then, with all his arrogance, with all his power, with all his wealth, and social prestige had to give up.

What was at stake was not just a matter of being annoyed by that woman: it was a matter of losing his credibility. The whole legal system was at risk. The lies of the unjust legal system were insistently being spread by the widow. She raised her voice in a culture where widows were taught to be quiet. The widow kept on putting her feet on the court, where women were forbidden to speak! The widow continued to fight for her rights in a system that commonly agreed not to do justice to the poor!

The judge had to give up because the boldness of this widow kept her protesting, no matter what! "In spite of everything," "even if it was at night."

Let me get it straight:
The civil rights movement rejected the saying: "nothing will change reality" because, like the bold widow of this parable who defeated the powerful judge, the civil rights movement did change so many things! And it started by changing the very church hymns, for example:

"If you miss me from praying down here" was changed to "if you miss me from the back of the bus"/ "This little light of mine" to "This little light of freedom"/ "Woke up this morning with my mind on Jesus" to "woke up this morning with my mind on freedom"/ "When I'm in trouble Lord walk with me" to "Down in the jailhouse, Lord,

206

walk with me", "If you want to get to heaven" to "If you want to get your freedom."

Who knows, if the widow who fought for her rights were in St. Croix on these days of patriotism, maybe she would´ve made the distinction between greed and patriotism. Maybe she wouldn't sing: "America the Great", unless Virgin Islanders were allowed to vote during the presidential election. Maybe this widow wouldn't pay daily homage to the flag, unless the living expenses of the Virgin Islands were the same as for example the state of Illinois. Maybe this widow wouldn't buy in the mega stores, unless their workers were well paid and unionized. Maybe this widow wouldn't believe that the main problem of our time is the intoxication with anthrax, but poverty and hunger. Brazil is one of the main producers of food in the world and more than half of Brazilians are undernourished due to the lack of democracy in the distribution of bead.

This is the story of a widow who defeated the system of injustice, the story of a widow who left behind her the culture of silence and began lifting up her voice, telling the truth, transforming the world!

207

48
NO OTHER NAME?[72]
I Kings 21; Luke 23. 33-43; Acts 4.7-12

When my wife was teaching Spanish at Redan High School, Stony Mountain, Atlanta, se asked her students to call her "maestra", meaning female teacher. Immediately one teenager raised his protest: "Me ain't gonna call you 'maestra'; you're not my master!" The "Massa Jesus" and the "Yes Massa" are still alive!

The same ice feelings emerge when we talk about Jesus' royal titles such as Lord, Sovereign, King, Almighty, Majestic, etc. which have been associated with imperialism, colonization and the intolerance of: "there is no other name under heaven given among human beings by which we must be saved."

This Sunday is the end of the Christian Year, the season of ordinary time finishes this morning. We close the long journey with "Christ the King" feast, because the kingdom of God was the core of Jesus' message. Other Christian churches even go further by naming this celebration: "Jesus Christ, King of the Universe."

The challenge we have before us is how to honor Jesus Christ as King in a liberating way, cntrary to the history of political, economic and cultural oppression, by European and USA missionaries under the pretext of "Christ the King" or of "No other name."

Well, let me try three routes: Ahab & Jezebel; Peter & John; Africans & the West Indies.

I. No Other Name in Ahab & Jezebel
"Christ the king" is a troublesome title because of the strong

opposition the prophets of the Old Testament showed against the monarchy. To mention just one example, the monarchs Ahab and Jezebel illustrate the abusive policies of the crown. King Solomon didn't care about the hungry people of his reign, he only cared about playing with his monkey pet (1 Kings 22.2); King Ahab also didn't care about the famine that was killing his people, he only cared about feeding his horses and mules. (1 Kings 18.5)

The greedy king Ahab desired his neighbor's vineyard, but Naboth didn't agree to sell it because he knew that land in general was not for sale, it was something sacred, and because, most probably, it was his source for making a living. The other day I heard on the radio that what the King really wanted was to get rid of his neighbors and to live in isolation, in the lordly fashion, but that is "another enchilada!"

Queen Jezebel knew her business. She began by making a case of Naboth. She demonized the enemy of the crown with the charges of blasphemer to God and to the King. The religious leaders, the Supreme Court, the Army and the Media, also did their job, and Naboth was stoned to death, because, according to Jezebel there was no other name but Ahab! Among Aztec Indians democracy was for real: it was a common person (macehual) the one who stoned to death his "supreme speaker", or huey-tlatoani Moctezuma, inaccurately translated as emperor, when he favored the King of Spain and betrayed his people.

You see how embarrassing it is to call Christ king, with all this line of tyrant kings and lords?

We might as well go to our second illustration:

209

II. No Other Name in Peter and John

"Gold and silver I do not have, but I give you what I have; stand up and walk," said Peter. Later on the clergy were saying: "Gold and silver we have —but we have nothing to give."[73]

The New Testament history of the physically challenged man healed by Peter has been misused as the main source of Christian imperial colonization. When we hear the Europenized titles of king and lord for Jesus, that brings to our memories the way non-European and non-USA cultures were demonized. The Christian empire loved to picture Jesus as an emperor by quoting Peter's words: "there is no salvation in no one else, for there is no other name under heaven given among human beings by which we must be saved."

But this royalist way of interpreting Jesus misses the whole point. Peter's declaration about no other name took place in the story of the healing of a physically challenged man. In fact, to save means also to heal and to liberate. "No other name" also points to the truth that a name, in Jesus' culture wasn't an empty word. The name of a person pointed towards the very identity of that person. Exactly like my name Elisha, the name Jesus in Greek, or Joshua in Hebrew, consisted of two words meaning "Yahweh saves, heals, or liberates."

Therefore, instead of Peter preaching about Jesus as the only source of salvation, he preached about God as the only one who heals, saves and liberates in all cultures and in all ages!

Now, what does it mean:

III. No Other Name in the West Indies

Another problem with Christ's title of king is that it leaves out queens. Fortunately Virgin Islanders have a long tradition of rejecting the "no other name" or the "only men's club."

210

St. Croix has lots of queens, being the most famous three: the Antiguan Queen Mary; Queen Matilda and Queen Agnes. The Caribbean tradition of queenship was brought from Africa where women were the center of the family, around which everything revolved. In African culture, matriarchal women were in charge of social life and of feeding the family. In the Virgin Islands during the times of slavery, women were more empowered, as Lutheran historian Willocks writes: "A queen was chosen for each plantation or estate. She was usually noted for her skill, bravery, and intelligence, and presided at Christmas and New Year's celebrations. She was responsible for organizing the social affairs, and quelling domestic and estate problems among the slaves. She also exhibited great influence over not only the slaves of their own estate, but those on other plantations as well."[74] After the abolition of slavery, queens continued fighting for a more humane society, as we can see their leadership in the Fireburn labor riot of 1878 and in Saint Thomian Queen Coziah leading of the coal workers' strike in 1892 due to the Mexican silver crisis.

Let me put it this way:

We are closing the liturgical year with the feast of "Christ the King" but God's Kingdom is very different from the kingdoms of this world.

The kingdoms of this world are like the kingdom of Pilate. They use coercion, they impose their own will against the will of the people. Like Pilate, the kingdoms of this world promote arbitrariness, privileges, domination, and later, in a very hypocritical way they wash their hands! The Roman soldiers and the "bad criminal" are tempting Jesus to use his power in a selfish way, for their own advantage, following the absolutistic "no other name" fashion.

The Kingdom of God is a Kingdom of love, of justice, of caring, of tenderness, as we saw through our Caribbean queens, and as we have witnessed throughout the whole liturgical year which ends this Sunday. The "good criminal" has learned to see Christ the King not as the majestic "no other name" like Ahab and Jezebel, surrounded by their army, their priests, their media, stealing vineyards, lands, countries, killing people with massive weapons. No, the "good criminal" now sees Christ the king dying on the cross for taking sides with the excluded people of society and church.

211

"The good criminal" at the last minute got the point: "No other name" is far away from the enthroned world powers who keep on destroying poor countries; "no other name" is far from crowned tyrants who have hired preachers to bless their malicious policies: "we have no King but Cesar." (John 19.15) The "good criminal" now sees that "no other name" means that God is the only one who heals, who saves and who liberates in all cultures, not only in the Euro-American culture, and liberates in all ages, not only since the incarnation of Jesus Christ.

The "good criminal" is now in Paradise!

212

NOTES

Introduction

1. "Migajas homiléticas; el método teológico latino y la predicación." In Daniel Rodríguez Díaz - Rodolfo Espinosa Ceballos (eds.) *Pulpito cristiano y justicia social.* South Holland, Il.- Mexico, D.F.: El Faro - Borinquen, 1994.

2. "En la vida todo es ir" in *Concierto Acústico, Fiel a la Vega* disco III.

2. A New Age of History?

3. Handsard, *Three Series* LXXVII, 1290, 1292, 1302, Feb. 26, 1845. Quoted in, Eric Eustace Williams, *From Columbus to Castro: the History of the Caribbean* 1492-1969. New York: Vintage Books, 1984, 194.

3. *Umbumwe:* the Communion of the Saints

4. Søren Kierkegaard, (*Papirer* X 4 A 246 n.d. 1851) (*Journals and Papers.* 600. Edited and translated by Howard V. Hong and Edna H. Hong, 7 vols. Bloomington and London: Indiana University Press, 1967-78.

6. Sophia's Feast!

5. I apologize for not being able to provide this reference at this moment.

7. He Took, Blessed, Broke and Gave Bread!

6. Here I'm following some of the steps of John Dominic Crossan, *Jesus: A Revolutionary Biography.* New York: Harper Collins, 1994, 179 ff.

7. Kikuo Matsunga. "Is John's gospel anti-sacramental? A new solution in light of the Evangelist's milieu," *in New Testament Studies* vol. 27, 516-24. Juan Bek shared this precious essay with me.

8. Eddie Donoghue. "Famine, epidemics, depleted Danish West Indian slave population." # 49 (Oct. 8-9, 2000) It is a shame that St. Croix's *Avis* is not publishing any more the powerful section of this scholar, from whom I have profited a lot.

10. Let's Talk Turkey!

9. Norman Perrin. *Rediscovering the Teaching of Jesus.* New York: Harper & Row, 1967, 102-107.

10. Crossan, *Op. Cit.*, 68.

11. Jack Weatherford. *Indian Givers: How The Indians of the Americas Transformed the World.* New York: Fawcett Columbine, 1990, 63 ff.

12. *Ibid, 69.*

13. Carlos Fuentes. *The Buried Mirror: Reflections on Spain and the New World.* New York: Houghton Mifflin, 1992, 205-06.

14. Weatherford, *Op. Cit.*

15. Charles Heiser. *Nightshades: The Paradoxical Plants.* San Francisco: W.H. Freeman, 1969.

12. The Right to Eat

16. N. Perrin, *Op. Cit.*

17. Rafael Aguirre. *La mesa compartida: estudios del Nuevo Testamento desde las ciencias sociales.* Santander: Sal Terrae, 1994, 28.

18. Daniela Romagnoli. "Mind your manners: Etiquette at the table," in Jean-Louis Flandrin and Massimo Montanari (eds). *Food: A Culinary History.* New York: Penguin Books, 1999, 331.

19. Paul de Rousiers. *La Vie américaine.* Paris: Firmin Didot, 1892. Cited by Claude Fischler, "McDonaldization of Culture," *Ibid*, 538.

20. François Houtart - François Polet (eds.) *El otro Davos; globalización de resistencias y luchas.* Madrid: Plaza y Valdes, n.d., 122.

13. Neither Greatness nor Servitude

21. Eddie Donoghue. "Suicide was more acceptable to the Aminas tribe than servitude" *The Avis*, St. Croix, # 44 (Sep. 3-4, 2000), 9.

22. David Katzman. *Seven Days a Week: Women and Domestic Service in Industrializing America.* New York: Oxford, 1978. Quoted by Jacquelyn Grant, "The Sin of Servanthood" 207. In Emilie M. Townes (ed). *A Troubling in my Soul: Womanist Perspective on Evil and Suffering.* Maryknoll, NY: Orbis, 1999, 149.

23. David Chidester. *Salvation and Suicide: An Interpretation of Jim Jones, the Peoples Temple, and Jonestown.* Bloomington and Indianapolis: Indiana University Press, 1991, 42, 167.

14. I Shall Not Want

24. Sidney W. Mintz. *Tasting Food, Tasting Freedom. Excursions into Eating, Culture and the Past.* Boston: Beacon Press, 1996, 64 ff.

16. St. Lazarous' Day and the Physically Challenged

25. William R. Herzog II. *Parables as Subversive Speech: Jesus as Pedagogue of the Oppressed.* Louisville, KY: Westminster/John Knox Press, 1994, 114-130.

17. The Woman Who Defeated Jesus

26. Martin Hengel. *Crucifixion.* Philadelphia: Fortress Press, 1977, 9.

18. "Not All that Glitters is Gold"

27. Eduardo Galeano, "América Latina a 30 años de la muerte del Che: democracias de baja intensidad, agresiones y resistencias." In Antonio Albiñana. *Geopolítica del caos.* Madrid: Le Monde Diplomatique, 1999, 27.
28. Houtart, *Op. Cit.*

19. Assault Upon the Temple

29. Mary Lou Thomsen called my attention to this fact.
30. Søren Kierkegaard. *The Moment and Late Writings.* Tr. Int. and notes by Howard and Edna Hong. Princeton, NJ: Princeton University Press, 1998, 245.
31. Bruce Kirmmse. *Kierkegaard in Golden Age Denmark.* Bloomington and Indianapolis: Indiana University Press, 1990, 79.
32. Søren Kierkegaard, *The Moment...* *Op. Cit.* 185.
33. Leonard Silk. *The New York Times,* September 30, 1983, 32.

20. Blind Belief

34. Edmundo O'Gorman, "Lecture on the Invention of America," Claustro de Tlatelolco, Mexico, D.F., October, 18, 1989.
35. Albert Memmi. *Retrato del colonizado.* Buenos Aires: Ediciones de la Flor, 1996.
36. Crossan, *Op. Cit.* 33 ff.
37. Memmi, *Op. Cit.* 83, 88.
38. Isabel Piquer, "Estados Unidos regresa al mundo de la fantasía con el centenario de Walt Disney," *El País*, December 6, 2001.

23. Can Anything Good Come from Nazareth?

39. Søren Kierkegaard. *Practice in Christianity.* Int. tr. and notes by Howard and Edna Hong. Princeton, NJ: Princeton University Press, 1991, 43-44.
40. Cecil Alexander 1823-1895, "All Things Bright and Beautiful."
41. Jean-Bertrand Aristide. *In the Parish of the Poor: Writings from Haiti.* Maryknoll, NY: Orbis, 1991, 90.

24. The Sacred Family

42. Leonard Swidler. *Biblical Affirmations of Women.* Philadelphia: Fortress Press, 1979, 59.

26. Epiphany Feast!

43. Franz J. Hinkelammer. *Sacrificios humanos y sociedad Occidental: Lucifer y la Bestia.* San José, Costa Rica: DEI, 1991, 37.

27. Touching, Lifting, Laying Hands and Blessing

44. Crossan, *Op. Cit.* 63 ff.

29. My Lord's A-writtin' all the Time

45. Leopoldo Zea, *Anthropos* # 89 (1988) 27.

215

30. We Are Star Powder!

46. I heard this illustration from Dr. José David Rodríguez Rivera, who was quoting Dr. Ángel M. Mergal.
47. José Míguez Bonino shared this with me during his visit to Puerto Rico by the end of 1998.

31. Are You Really God's Daughter?

48. Chidester, *Op. Cit.* 175.
49. Harold W. Willocks. *The Umbilical Cord: The History of the United States Virgin Islands from Pre-Columbiana Era to the Present.* Christiansted, V.I.: n.p., 1995, 212.

32. Nicodemus and Civil Disobedience

50. Gonzalo Aguirre Beltrán. *El negro esclavo en Nueva España.* Mexico, D.F.: Fondo de Cultura Económica, 1994, 179 ff.
51. Decio Freitas Palmares. *A guerra dos escravos.* Porto Alegre-RS: Mercado Abierto, 1984, 29.
52. Robert Michael Franklin. *Liberating Visions: Human Fulfillment & Social Justice in African-American Thought.* Minneapolis, MN: Fortress Press, 1990, 134.

33. The God Who Forgives Economic Debts

53. Laura Esquivel. *Like Water for Chocolate.* New York: Anchor Book, 1992.

34. The For-Giving God

54. Søren Kierkegaard. *Practice... Op. Cit.* 19-20.

35. The Reshaping of Society

55. Desmond Tutu. *Esperanza y sufrimiento; sermones y discursos.* Grand Rapids: Eerdmans, 1988, 150.
56. Martin Luther King's last sermon.

36. We Be Jammin!

57. Vine Deloria. *God is Red: A Native View of Religion.* Colorado: Fulcrum Publishing, 1992, 227.
58. I heard Dr. Salatiel Palomino López preaching on these two texts on Easter 1997.

37. The Resurrection From Below

59. Jürgen Moltmann. *The Source of Life: the Holy Spirit and the Theology of Life.* Minneapolis: Fortress Press, 1997, 123.

39. Jesus' Promotion to the Hall of Fame

60. I thank Justo L. González for this and many more intuitions.

40. Let's Get Together and Feel Alright!

61. "Doriangreyism," coined by Dr. Salatiel Palomino López.

216

41. The African Who Sponsored Jesus Christ

62. Luis Alonso-Schökel. *Celebrating the Eucharist: Biblical Meditations.* New York: Crossroad, 1989, 9-10.

42. Can't You Preach?

63. Willocks, *Op. Cit.* 38.

64. I'm very appreciative of José David Rodríguez Hernández, for sharing with me his valuable research. Cf. Gustav Sigfrid Swensson, "I Went to Puerto Rico," *El Testigo* (Octubre 1948), 16. Cited by José D. Rodríguez, "In search for the Messiah in the mission field" in *Currents in Theology and Mission* 28:3-4 (June/August 2001).

43. Silencing the Past

65. I borrowed this title from prophetic Hatian scholar Michel-Rolph Trouillot. *Silencing the Past: Power and the Production of History.* Boston, Massachusetts: Beacon Press, 1995.

44. St Martin of Tours

66. Hinkelammert, *Sacrificios... Op. Cit.* 169 ff.

45. Get Up and Walk!

67. Søren Kierkegaard. *Letter* 30 [1847] Villads Christensen. In *Letters and Documents.* Int. tr. and notes by Henry Rosenmeier. New Jersey: Princeton University Press, 1978.

68. *Letter* 150 [1847] Henriette Kierkegaard (JP 6063).

69. *Letter* 167 [December 1847] Henriette Kierkegaard.

70. Walter Altmann, "Justification in a Context of Exclusion - Latin America," in Wolfang Grieve (ed.) *Justification in the World's Context.* Geneva: The Lutheran World Federation, 2000, 120.

71. Meric Casaubon. *Credulity & Incredulity: In things Divine & Spiritual...* London: 8vo. TN for Samuel Lownds, 1672, 71.

48. No Other Name?

72. George E. "Tink" Tinker, Homer Noley and Clara Sue Kidwell. *A Native Theology.* Maryknoll, NY: Orbis, 2001, 76 ff.

73. Søren Kierkegaard, (Pap. X 1 A 672 n.d., 1849) (JP, 384)

74. Willocks, *Op. Cit.* 212.

217

Old Testament References

Genesis

3.19 131, 132
16.6 176

Exodus

20.4 33
22.22-24 204
23:16, 34:22 175
34.29 154

Leviticus

12.1-5 122
12.6-8 122

Numbers

11.4-9, 21.4-9 16
21.4-9 16, 139

Deuteronomy

8.2-5 136
8.3 63
24.17 204

Judges

4.5 154
14 59
19.4 60

1 Samuel

2.1-11 3

2. Samuel

6.16-23 157, 158

1 Kings

17.1-24 73
17.10-16 155
18.5 209
19.12 155
21 208
22.2 209

2 Kings

1.2 154
22.14 154

Psalms

113 3
22.16,20 71
23 59, 78, 79
95.5 33

Proverbs

9 24, 25
9.1-6 24
9.3 25
15.17 17

Isaiah

2.4 62
9.5 169
35.5-6, 61.1-2 89
40.11 200
65.22 9

New Testament References

Matthew

2.1-11 111
2.13-23 107
3.1-12 81
4 109

9.1 104
11.2-11 86
11.11 93
17.1-9 153
18.25 177
20. 1-16 51

21.1-11 157
21.9 158
21.13 82
25 19, 39, 64, 178,
191, 194

Index

C

Cairo 116
Calvin, John 189
Camara, Helder 64, 155
Cameran, Glenroy 116, 120
Canary Islands 18
Carpentier, Alejo 188
Casaldáliga, Pedro 155
Casaubon, Meric 217
Celsus 95
Claude A., Benjamin 101, 167, 171
Colombia 38, 113, 203
Colón, Diego 80
Colorado 62
Columbus 18, 107, 152, 180, 183
Constantine 29, 179
Copenhagen 10, 83, 183
Costa Rica 113
Coziah, Queen 137, 211
Crittenden, Evelyn 165
Crossan, John Dominic 213, 215
Cuba 66, 69, 78, 97, 102, 136, 188, 189, 202
Cudjoe 142
Cuencas, Jaheem 116, 120
Cyrene 15, 179, 180, 181, 182

CH

Chidester, David 214, 216
Chile 113
China 17, 164
Christian, Barbara 101, 129
Christian, Elena 27

D

Danneskjold Laurving, Ferdinand 183
David, Ché 51
Davis, Dolorita 25, 165

Davis, Olasse 101
Dead Sea 34
Decapolis 35
Deloria, Vine 216
Denmark 3, 5, 6, 10, 83, 107, 138, 151, 192, 196, 198
Denver 40, 165
Diderot, Denis 45
Disney, Walt 84, 90
Dominican Republic 14, 18, 39, 50, 100, 113, 202
Donnella, Joshep 125
Donoghue, Eddie 213, 214
Drake, Sir Francis 17, 45
Duncan, Tim 171

E

Egypt 16, 38, 108, 136, 157, 180, 182, 203
El Salvador 150, 202
England 5, 10, 23, 43, 45, 46, 68, 100, 194, 207
Erhard, Ludwig 192
Espinosa Ceballos, Rodolfo 213
Esquivel, Laura 216
Europe 4, 5, 6, 17, 19, 25, 38, 40, 43, 44, 45, 46, 50, 71, 79, 100, 105, 117, 123, 124, 128, 130, 183, 189, 190, 208, 210

F

Falucho 142
Fanon, Frantz 174, 189
Fatiman, Cécile 142
Feliciano, José 36
Fox, Vicente 148, 151
France 5, 46, 62, 89, 174
Francis, Emma 165
Francis, Rothschild 101, 142, 168, 170

222

223

224

225

226

Esta edición consta de 1000 ejemplares más sobrantes para reposición, y se terminó de imprimir en el mes de marzo del año 2002, en los talleres de Jiménez Editores, Callejón de la Luz No. 32-20, Col. Anáhuac, México, D.F. Se utilizó la familia de letra New Times Roman, papel de interiores cultural de 90 kgs., papel del forro cartulina sulfatada de 12 ptos., laminado en mate. El cuidado de la edición estuvo a cargo de Rodolfo Espinosa Ceballos.